DRAMA CLASSICS

The Drama Classics series aims to offer the world's greatest plays in affordable paperback editions for students, actors and theatregoers. The hallmarks of the series are accessible introductions, uncluttered texts and an overall theatrical perspective.

Given that readers may be encountering a particular play for the first time, the introduction seeks to fill in the theatrical/historical background and to outline the chief themes rather than concentrate on interpretational and textual analysis. Similarly the play-texts themselves are free of footnotes and other interpolations: instead there is an end-glossary of 'difficult' words and phrases.

The texts of the English language plays in the series have been prepared taking full account of all existing scholarship. The foreign-language plays have been newly translated into a modern English that is both actable and accurate: many of the translators regularly have their work staged professionally.

Edited until his early death by Kenneth McLeish, the Drama Classics series continues with his aim of providing a first-class library of dramatic literature representing the best of world theatre.

Associate editors:
Professor Trevor R. Griffiths
Dr. Colin Counsell
School of Arts and Humanities
University of North London

DRAMA CLASSICS *the first hundred*

*The publishers welcome
suggestions for further
titles*

DRAMA CLASSICS

UNCLE VANYA

by
Anton Chekhov

translated and with an introduction by
Stephen Mulrine

NICK HERN BOOKS
London
www.nickhernbooks.co.uk

A Drama Classic

Uncle Vanya first published in Great Britain in this translation
as a paperback original in 1999 by Nick Hern Books Limited,
14 Larden Road, London W3 7ST. Reprinted 2006

Typeset by Country Setting, Kingsdown, Kent CT14 8ES
Printed by Bookmarque, Croydon, Surrey

A CIP catalogue record for this book is available from
the British Library

ISBN-10: 1 85459 430 3 / ISBN-13   978 1 85459 430 3

Introduction

Anton Chekhov (1860–1904)

Anton Pavlovich Chekhov was born in Taganrog, a seaport in South Russia, in 1860. By his own account, his childhood was far from idyllic. His father Pavel was a domestic tyrant, fanatically religious, and Chekhov and his brothers were forced to rise before dawn to sing in the local church choir, then work long hours after school, in the family grocer's shop.

Taganrog was in decline, but its Greek shipping community was relatively wealthy, and Chekhov was first sent to a Greek-language school, which his father naively regarded as the highway to a lucrative career. After a wasted year, Chekhov was enrolled in the local high school, where he stayed, an unremarkable scholar, until 1879.

His last years at the Taganrog school were spent apart from his family, however, since his bankrupt father had fled to Moscow, where Chekhov's elder brothers were already students. Chekhov completed his studies, entered Moscow University's Faculty of Medicine, and at the age of nineteen became the family's principal breadwinner, writing short comic pieces to supplement his student allowance.

By the time he qualified in 1884, Chekhov's literary ambitions were already in conflict with what he regarded as his true vocation. Indeed, until his own health collapsed, he continued to practise medicine, mostly as an unpaid service to nearby rural communities. Chekhov was almost certainly infected with tuberculosis from childhood, and the disease was in its terminal stages before he would permit an independent diagnosis. In addition to frequent haemorrhaging from the lungs, which forced him to spend the winters in the warm South, Chekhov also suffered from a variety of other chronic ailments, yet his work rate was little short of heroic. In 1899, when he agreed to sell the rights in his works to the publisher Marks, they already filled ten volumes, and the critical consensus is that his short stories are an unparalleled achievement, with the three great plays of his mature dramatic method, *Uncle Vanya*, *Three Sisters*, and *The Cherry Orchard*, no less important.

Human relationships are the substance of all Chekhov's work, and it is perhaps no surprise that this most intimate of writers remained elusive in his own. Although fond of women, and pursued by several, Chekhov characteristically retreated as they advanced, and it is a reasonable assumption that the happiness of his brief married life, with the actress Olga Knipper, depended to an extent on the lengthy periods of separation forced on the couple by the dramatist's poor health, and Olga's busy metropolitan career.

Finally, in a despairing effort to postpone the inevitable, Chekhov travelled with Olga to Germany for medical treatment. In July 1904, following a heart attack, he died in the spa town of Badenweiler, at the age of forty-four.

Uncle Vanya: **What Happens in the Play**

In common with all Chekhov's mature plays, *Uncle Vanya* begins with an arrival and ends with a departure; it is the record of a visit, in effect, during which the temporary guests contrive to disrupt the settled routine of the residents. In *Uncle Vanya*, this disturbance happens at the mundane level of family mealtimes and work schedules, but more damagingly at an emotional level, resulting in the familiar Chekhovian 'merry-go-round' of unrequited love, which gives the play its forward movement and power.

The action takes place in the country house of Professor Serebryakov, a retired academic, who suffers from chronic ill-health, and who has now returned, after many years, to his first wife's estate, accompanied by his second wife, Yelena Andreyevna, much younger than himself and an acknowledged beauty. As the play opens, Dr Astrov, a local physician and amateur environmentalist, is reminiscing with the old family nurse, Marina, when they are joined first by Voinitsky, the eponymous 'Uncle Vanya', then Serebryakov and Yelena, who have been out walking with Sonya, the Professor's daughter by his first wife, who was Vanya's sister, and their house-guest, Telegin.

Serebryakov retreats to his room, and in his absence Vanya is cynically dismissive of the Professor's academic

pretensions, and his young wife's fidelity to him,
upsetting both Telegin, and his own mother, who still
dotes on Serebryakov. Dr Astrov, we learn, has had a
wasted journey, having been summoned to attend the
Professor, who now peevishly refuses to see him, but
before Astrov leaves he delivers an impassioned speech
on his pet subject, tree-planting and forest conservation.
Yelena at first appears bored, and Sonya, who is secretly
in love with Astrov, springs to his defence. It is clear,
though, that Yelena is intrigued by Astrov himself, if not
by his cause. As the first act ends, however, with Yelena
and Vanya left alone, the latter declares his love for
Yelena, who reacts with a show of irritation.

The mood of irritation is continued in the second act, as
Serebryakov, unable to sleep, launches into a torrent of
complaint to Yelena, who feels that he is obscurely
blaming her for being young and healthy, while his own
life is almost over. Sonya and Marina eventually
persuade Serebryakov to go to bed, and Vanya, again left
alone with Yelena, and emboldened by drink, challenges
her to justify her sham marriage, and the morality of
remaining faithful to a self-pitying, egocentric tyrant.
Yelena storms out of the room, and Vanya is then joined
by Telegin and Dr Astrov. Astrov, who has also been
drinking, teases Vanya about his interest in the
Professor's young wife, until they are interrupted by the
returning Sonya, who rebukes them for their unseemly
behaviour.

Vanya goes out, leaving Astrov with Sonya, who seizes
the opportunity to test Astrov's feelings for her,

questioning him obliquely about love, and how he might react to an approach by a hypothetical 'sister'. Astrov's response is not encouraging, and the unhappy Sonya is left to reflect on the fact that she is too plain to interest him. Yelena then enters, and the two women come to a tearful understanding, in which Yelena confesses her own unhappiness.

At the beginning of the third act, the family are assembled to await the Professor, who has an important announcement to make. Sonya mildly rebukes Yelena for the idle life she leads, and the way in which her languor seems to have infected not only Vanya, but even Dr Astrov. Sonya ends by confessing her love for Astrov, and Yelena offers to quiz him on her behalf, to find out once and for all what her prospects are. Yelena then asks Astrov to show her his charts, on which he has recorded the environmental harm done, over the past fifty years, by uncontrolled deforestation. She affects to be interested, but eventually admits to her true purpose. It is quite clear that Astrov has no feeling for Sonya, and he agrees to cease visiting the house, to spare her further pain. However, Astrov shrewdly detects the real motives behind Yelena's 'interrogation', and when he attempts to kiss her, her resistance is easily overcome. At that point, Vanya appears, and catches sight of them embracing.

A very awkward situation is interrupted by the entry of Serebryakov, who proceeds to outline his grand plan to the assembled family: basically, he intends to sell off his first wife's estate, invest the capital, and live off the interest. Vanya, already in emotional disarray, can scarcely believe his ears. Legally, the estate belongs to his niece Sonya, alongside whom he has worked tirelessly for years, sending the Professor the profits of their labours, to support his academic ambitions. Vanya believes they are now to be cast aside, and explodes in a rage, before rushing from the room. Serebryakov follows him out, and a shot is heard. Vanya has tried to shoot the Professor, and when they re-enter, he fails in a second attempt.

Serebryakov and Yelena obviously cannot remain in the house, and the fourth act begins with the preparations for their departure. Astrov and Vanya engage in some verbal sparring, on the subject of the Professor's wife, but there is a serious edge to it, and Astrov eventually asks Vanya to return the bottle of morphia he has taken from his medical bag. Vanya at first denies all knowledge of it, but under pressure from Sonya, he hands the morphia back, and the crisis is over. Yelena and Astrov then bid each other a tense farewell, in which Astrov reflects on how she has bewitched them all, and she coyly admits her own infatuation with him. Serebryakov and Vanya next make peace, and as the Professor and his wife leave, followed by Astrov soon afterwards, life for Sonya and Uncle Vanya returns to a normality of sorts, as they crouch over the estate account books, choking back their despair.

Chekhov the Dramatist

Chekhov might be described as the writer's writer, not only on account of his work, or the fund of wisdom in his correspondence, but also the example he presents of the tireless self-improver, grinding his way over a mere two decades from penny-a-line squibs in the comic papers, to the status of modern classic, in both his preferred genres.

In that respect, the year 1887-88 represents a turning-point in his career, with the staging of his first four-act play, *Ivanov* (leaving aside the unplayable epic now known as *Platonov*), and the publication of his short story *The Steppe* in one of the prestige 'thick journals', 'The Northern Herald'. The same year also saw his official recognition as a major Russian writer with the award of the Pushkin Prize, by the Academy of Sciences. Chekhov had arrived, it seems, though the reception given to *Ivanov*, premièred in Moscow to mixed cheering and booing, suggested he had done so some way ahead of his audience.

That is broadly the story of Chekhov's dramatic career, and it is significant that the main bone of contention in *Ivanov*, dividing first-nighters into partisans and scoffers, was the author's seeming abdication of any clear moral stance. After some changes, however, the play was successfully revived in St. Petersburg, and Chekhov was emboldened to offer his next play, *The Wood Demon*, for production in Moscow the following year. Alas, *The Wood Demon* was a flop, and in the light of Chekhov's developing method, it is interesting to note that criticism generally centred on its lack of action, and dreary slice-of-life dialogue. Chekhov withdrew the play in disgust, and buried it deep within his mysterious creative processes, whence it emerged in 1897, in the radically altered form of *Uncle Vanya*, one of the greatest works of the modern theatre.

Between times, Chekhov endured the catastrophic failure of *The Seagull*, an experience which encapsulated everything that was wrong with the Russian theatre of his day, and which his work did so much to change. *The Seagull* was premièred in October 1896 at the Alexandrinsky Theatre in St. Petersburg, which in Chekhov's day was both the administrative and cultural capital of the country, and it was especially important that his new venture should succeed there. Unfortunately, the play spent almost a year in the hands of the censors, which meant that the actors received their scripts a bare week before opening night. Worse still, *The Seagull* had been commissioned from Chekhov as a vehicle for the benefit performance of one of the Alexandrinsky's stars, Levkeyeva, a mature comedienne with a large and vociferous following. She had originally been billed to play Arkadina, but had decided instead to appear in a three-act comedy, ironically titled *This Happy Day*, to be staged immediately after *The Seagull*. The disappointment of her fans, forced to endure four acts of Chekhov, is thus not difficult to imagine, and the play was accompanied with whistling and jeering almost from its opening lines.

After the fiasco of *The Seagull*, Chekhov fled from St. Petersburg, and although the play's fortunes improved with 'normal' audiences, the generally hostile reviews made him resolve to quit the theatre for ever. Fortunately, the first great play of his maturity as a dramatist, *Uncle Vanya*, appears to have been already on the stocks, and while the course of its development out of *The Wood Demon* remains unclear, it almost certainly followed the writing of *The Seagull*. At any rate, *Uncle Vanya* first surfaced in 1897, when Chekhov had it published.

The following year, 1898, saw the coming together of Chekhov and the newly-founded Moscow Art Theatre – a meeting commonly presented as a marriage made in theatre heaven. Its founders, Stanislavsky and Nemirovich-Danchenko, shared Chekhov's dissatisfaction with the Russian theatre of the day, its bombastic acting, poor technical standards, and outmoded star system. Stanislavsky, a wealthy merchant's son, ran his own amateur theatre company, and Nemirovich-Danchenko lectured in drama at the Moscow Philharmonic School, where his students included Olga Knipper, eventually to become Chekhov's wife, and the future director Vsevolod Meyerhold.

The Moscow Art Theatre was the product of their determination to create a new kind of professional theatre, in which the ensemble, rather than the individual actor, would be paramount, and which would pay close attention not only to the text, but also to scenery, costumes, lighting, incidental music and sound effects – even the design of the programme and the colour of the curtain. There were to be no 'benefit' performances, and no stars; the repertoire, Nemirovich-Danchenko's responsibility, would be chosen on literary merit alone, and an actor might play the lead in one production, and carry a spear in the next; in Stanislavsky's famous dictum: 'There are no small parts, only small actors'. The new company also had a mission to educate audiences to a proper respect for the drama, and even excluded latecomers – unheard of in the commercial theatre of the day.

What Chekhov's plays needed – natural, unforced speaking, even-handed ensemble playing and lengthy, painstaking rehearsal – appeared to be exactly what the Moscow Art Theatre could bring to them, and indeed it is debatable how much of Stanislavsky's famous 'method' was developed from Chekhov's writing. And if the relationship turned out to be less than wholly blissful, it is to their credit nonetheless, that Chekhov continued to write for the stage, including the two masterpieces specially commissioned by the Moscow Art Theatre, *Three Sisters* and *The Cherry Orchard*.

The rapturous reception accorded to *The Seagull* at its Moscow première on 17 December 1898, has passed into legend. Its success not only restored Chekhov's confidence, it also rescued the fortunes of the Moscow Art Theatre, who were now eager to attempt *Uncle Vanya*, which had already been staged in the provinces. Unfortunately, Chekhov had promised the play to the Maly Theatre, but a number of script changes being demanded by its literary committee gave him a legitimate excuse for withdrawing the offer. *Uncle Vanya* was thus produced by the Moscow Art Theatre in October 1899 – in terms of its reception, more consolidation than triumph, but sufficiently encouraging to focus Chekhov's mind on a new subject – the lives of three sisters in a remote provincial town.

Three Sisters opened in January 1901, and while it was certainly no failure, neither it, nor *The Cherry Orchard* three years later, managed to repeat the smash hit of *The Seagull*. By the spring of 1903, when he began committing *The Cherry Orchard* to paper, Chekhov had little more than a year to live, and his health had deteriorated to such an extent that he could write only a few lines a day. Nonetheless, he was able to attend rehearsals at the Moscow Art Theatre in December, and *The Cherry Orchard* was premièred on Chekhov's forty-fourth birthday, 17 January, 1904. Three months later, Chekhov was dead, and the brief span of his career as a dramatist complete. We can only guess at what he might have achieved, had he lived as long as Ibsen, say, but in a mere handful of plays, Chekhov has given the classic repertoire not only a unique vision, but also, in his off-centre, low-key rhetoric, one of its most compelling modern voices.

Uncle Vanya and *The Wood Demon*

Chekhov's first success in the theatre was *Ivanov*, premièred in Moscow on 4 November, 1887, and its morally inert idealist-hero, who eventually shoots himself in despair, is a familiar figure in the later plays.

However, although *Ivanov* made enough of an impact to be taken up by the Alexandrinsky Theatre in St. Petersburg the following year, Chekhov himself was un-happy with the play, which was frankly melodramatic – part of the reason for its success, no doubt – observing theatrical conventions he was soon to abandon.

It is with *The Wood Demon*, written in late 1889, that Chekhov attempts a new kind of drama, one in which the critical events take place off-stage, while the characters get on with the humdrum business of living. *The Wood Demon* can now be seen as a transitional work, however, and its rejection by the Imperial theatres, before a Moscow actors' co-operative offered to produce it, was not entirely due to its innovative character, or the fact that it offended contemporary mores by its disrespectful treatment of a university professor. The Abramova Theatre production opened on 27 December, but by mid-January of 1890 it was already losing money, and was taken off. Chekhov was deeply disappointed, but in truth, the criticism of friend and foe alike, that *The Wood Demon* was a novel manqué, still holds good, and a comparison with *Uncle Vanya* shows not only how much work remained to be done, but also how expertly Chekhov managed the task.

Chekhov, who once advised a novice writer to take a pair of scissors to the first and last paragraphs, sight unseen, of his short story, cut *The Wood Demon* with surgical precision, and the nature of the cuts is instructive. While almost every character in *Uncle Vanya* already figures in *The Wood Demon*, though Astrov and Vanya appear as

Khrushchev and Uncle Georges, the earlier play has
several additional roles, which function as virtual
'shadows' of Serebryakov, Sonya, Astrov, and Vanya
himself. Chekhov's extra characters, the Zheltyukhins
and the Orlovskys, thicken the play's texture, but they
also blur its focus, and their excision streamlines the plot
of *Uncle Vanya*, as does its revised setting, reduced from
three different estates to one only, that of Serebryakov.

All the plot ingredients of *Uncle Vanya* are present in
The Wood Demon: the conflict between Serebryakov and
Vanya; the latter's infatuation with the Professor's young
wife; Sonya's troubled love for the environmentalist-
doctor; Yelena's coy interest in him. Much of the
incident is also common to both plays: the doctor and
Vanya engage in a dispute about forest conservation;
Vanya makes a clumsy pass at Yelena; someone walks in
on an apparent embrace; Serebryakov outlines his
scheme to sell off the estate; Vanya exits in a rage, and
an off-stage pistol shot is heard. In fact, almost the
entire content of Acts II and III of *Uncle Vanya* is
recycled from *The Wood Demon*. The difference is that the
sequence of events is now purposefully connected, and
the obscuring detail cut away. In *The Wood Demon*, for
example, it is the doctor, Khrushchev, and not Uncle
Georges, who chances upon what he interprets as a
lovers' tryst, but which is quite innocent, certainly on
Yelena's part. However, Uncle Georges' suicidal
depression, which culminates in the fatal pistol shot, is
later revealed to have been partly fuelled by the
slanderous rumours circulating about his relationship
with the Professor's wife.

That revelation is made in Act IV of *The Wood Demon*, through a narrated account of the discovery of Uncle Georges' diary, and Chekhov would never again employ so transparently unconvincing a device. Given that Act III closes on a genuinely tragic note, the picnic atmosphere of Act IV is also discordant, and the formulaic happy ending, in which three couples are paired off or re-united, including Sonya and her 'wood demon' doctor, is almost farcical. Chekhov here is scarcely recognisable, and this conclusion to the play is generally explained by the influence of Tolstoy. Indeed, almost the only enthusiast for *The Wood Demon* in Chekhov's own day was the Tolstoyan disciple Prince Urusov, who repeatedly urged him to publish it, regardless of its failure in the theatre. Chekhov's response, even ten years on, in a letter dated 16 October, 1899, could scarcely have been more emphatic:

> I can't publish *The Wood Demon*. I hate this play and I'm trying to forget it. Whether it's the fault of the piece itself, or the circumstances in which it was written and staged, I don't know, but it would be a real blow to me if it were somehow forcibly dragged into the light of day and revived.

The most penetrating critique of *The Wood Demon* is of course Chekhov's own, in the form of the great work which it eventually became. Among the more important changes, the 'reversal' of the interrupted embrace, in which it is now Vanya, clutching his peace-offering of autumn roses, who walks in on Astrov, is at once both comical, and inexpressibly poignant. The genius of the mature Chekhov is shown again in the scene of the off-stage pistol shot. Given Vanya's state of mind, we have every reason to expect suicide, so that when he re-enters in pursuit of Serebryakov, the shock is palpable. In that context, Vanya's outburst of 'Bang! Missed? Missed again!?' is funny, of course, but painful to behold – the unedifying spectacle of a man so inept that not even a gun in his hand can give him an advantage.

Chekhov's most radical alteration, however, was to discard Act IV of *The Wood Demon* almost completely, and the new, much shorter Act IV of *Uncle Vanya* is a masterpiece of anti-climax. There is a reconciliation of sorts, but it is very far from Tolstoyan. Serebryakov and Yelena go off to continue their half-life in grimy Kharkov, while Vanya and Sonya undertake to slave for them as before, and the brief, tantalising glimmer of hope, or any prospect of change, is extinguished forever. Chekhov's Act IV is as close to music as drama gets, with its studied recapitulation of themes and sustained diminuendo. Sonya's long closing speech, consoling Vanya, and herself, with a vision of an after-life in which they will at last find rest, is like an aria, but it is sung to the accompaniment not only of Telegin's guitar, but also the nightwatchman's tapping, Marina's knitting-needles, and Maria Vasilievna's demented scribbling, as she annotates her absurd pamphlets, diluting any hope it offers.

Ironically, but for the persistence of Urusov, who appears to have been besotted by *The Wood Demon*, Chekhov might well have succeeded in trying to forget it; it is our great good fortune that he did not, and *Uncle Vanya* is perhaps the most concentrated of all his plays, with its arrow-straight plot, and emotional power.

Uncle Vanya in Performance

Chekhov published *Uncle Vanya* in a collection of his plays in 1897, but the invitation to submit it to the prestige Maly Theatre did not come until February 1899. Meanwhile, it had been staged in a number of provincial towns, including Kiev, Odessa, and Tiflis, and been generally well received. When the script changes requested by the Maly authorities proved unacceptable, Stanislavsky and Nemirovich-Danchenko eagerly acquired the rights for the Moscow Art Theatre, and promised Chekhov it would be performed exactly as he had written it. This turned out to be less than the whole truth, and Stanislavsky indeed believed Chekhov to be a poor interpreter of his own works. Chekhov for his part thought Stanislavsky, in the role of Astrov, completely misunderstood the nature of his relationship with Yelena, and failed to convey his ironic detachment. The Moscow Art Theatre's obsession with naturalistic detail and sound effects also disturbed him, and while the introduction of live chickens, barking dogs, chirruping crickets, etc., could be classed as a minor irritant, Stanislavsky also added a piano duet for Yelena and Sonya, defeating Chekhov's purpose in the symbolism of the silent piano.

Chekhov's criticisms, however, tended to be expressed obliquely, and often in the form of costume notes – his insistence that Vanya should wear a silk necktie, for example, was a coded instruction on how the character should be played, that is, as an elegant, cultured man, not a stereotyped provincial. Chekhov also bore with some fortitude Stanislavsky's treatment of his dialogue, in which the effect of significant pauses, marked as such in the script, was diminished by the snail's-pace approach the Moscow Art Theatre believed his work required.

At any rate, *Uncle Vanya* opened in Moscow on 26 October, 1899, and although the production failed to repeat the success of *The Seagull*, it did well enough to interest the Alexandrinsky Theatre in St. Petersburg. *Uncle Vanya* also remained a fixture in the Moscow Art Theatre repertoire until the late 1920's, when Chekhov's drama entered on a long period of neglect, falling as it did beyond the narrow ideological bounds of Socialist Realism. In 1958, the Moscow Art Theatre toured three major plays to the UK, including *Uncle Vanya*, which had a profound influence on later British productions. The Moscow Art Theatre also revisited *Uncle Vanya* in an important production by Oleg Yefremov in 1985, and a filmed version of the play, directed by Andrei Konchalovsky in 1972, with Sergei Bondarchuk as Astrov, and Innokenty Smoktunovsky as Vanya, is regarded as one of the finest cinematic adaptations of Chekhov.

In the UK, the first English staging of *Uncle Vanya* at the Aldwych in 1914 was greeted with bewilderment for the most part, and it was not until 1926, with the emigré Fyodor Komisarjevsky's production, that the play made any real impact on English audiences, though the emphasis was on the lachrymose, rather than the comic. *Uncle Vanya* was given another notable outing in 1945, by the Old Vic Company, with Laurence Olivier as Astrov, Margaret Leighton as Yelena, and Ralph Richardson as Vanya, but while the production was much admired, the star-studded cast apparently found it difficult to submerge themselves fully in Chekhov's demanding ensemble.

Olivier, again playing Astrov, directed a production for the newly-founded National Theatre in 1963, with Michael Redgrave as Vanya, and worthy of note also is the Royal Court production of 1970, with Paul Scofield as Vanya and Colin Blakely as Astrov. The UK première of *The Wood Demon*, incidentally, was staged at the Arts Theatre, Cambridge, in 1973, with Ian McKellen as Khrushchev. Two major productions of *Uncle Vanya* took place in 1982: at the National Theatre, with Michael Bryant and Dinsdale Landen, and Cherie Lunghi as Yelena, and at the Theatre Royal, Haymarket, with Donald Sinden, Ronald Pickup, and Sheila Gish. More recently, Mike Alfreds directed Ian McKellen as Vanya and Antony Sher as Astrov, in a version by Pam Gems at the National Theatre in 1992. Chekhov's masterly exercise in recycling thus continues to be an inexhaustible repertoire favourite.

The Translation

Literary Russian has undergone much less change since Chekhov's day than has English, and there is little justification for using a period style in translation, particularly with a writer whose declared aim was to bring conversation to the stage, the common speech of the educated classes of his day, uttered in more or less commonplace contexts. For ease of playing, I have also for the most part simplified the Russian polite mode of address, i.e., first name and patronymic, which English speakers sometimes find difficult. A guide to pronunciation follows the play.

For Further Reading

Among the several biographies of Chekhov, Ronald
Hingley's *A New Life of Chekhov*, Oxford University Press,
1976, is outstanding not only for its wealth of detail, but
also the care the author takes to disentangle the man
from the work. Maurice Valency's *The Breaking String*,
Oxford University Press, 1966, and David Magarshack's
The Real Chekhov, George Allen & Unwin, 1972, remain
among the most perceptive and readable studies of the
plays, while Nick Worrall's contribution to Methuen's
Writer-Files series: *File on Chekhov*, Methuen, 1986, is
both a compact introduction to Chekhov's theatre, and a
valuable source of review material. *Anton Chekhov
Rediscovered*, edited by Senderovich and Sendich, Russian
Language Journal, 1987, includes a comprehensive
bibliography of works in English relating to Chekhov,
and *A Chekhov Companion*, edited by Toby W. Clyman,
Greenwood Press, 1985, contains useful articles on
themes ranging from social conditions in late 19th-
century Russia, to the critical tradition, both native and
Western. Chekhov's reception in the West, over the
period roughly 1900-1945, is also documented in detail
by Viktor Emeljanow, in *Chekhov, the Critical Heritage*,
Routledge & Kegan Paul, 1981. Patrick Miles' excellent
Chekhov on the British Stage, Cambridge University Press,

1993, is a collection of essays by several hands, and contains a chronology of British productions of Chekhov up to 1991. Finally, Donald Rayfield's little book, *Chekhov's 'Uncle Vania' and 'The Wood Demon'*, Bristol Classical Press, 1995, is a fascinating demonstration of the dramatist as critic.

Chekhov: Key Dates

1860   Born 17 January in Taganrog, a port on the Sea of Azov.

1875   Father's grocery business fails, family flees to Moscow, leaving Chekhov behind.

1879   Completes his education at the local high school, and sets off for Moscow, to enter the Medical Faculty of Moscow University.

1880   First comic story published in 'The Dragonfly', a St. Petersburg weekly.

1884   Graduates from University, begins medical practice in Moscow. First symptoms of tuberculosis.

1885   Contributes short stories to the 'St. Petersburg Gazette' and 'New Time'.

1886   First collection: *Motley Tales*.

1887   Second collection: *In the Twilight*. First performance of *Ivanov* at Korsh's Theatre, Moscow, 19 November.

1888   First major story, *The Steppe*, published in the 'Northern Herald'. Awarded Pushkin Prize for Literature, by the Imperial Academy of Sciences.

1889   First performance of *The Wood Demon* at Abramova's Theatre, Moscow, 27 December.

1890   Travels across Siberia to carry out research on the penal colony of Sakhalin Island.

1896   Disastrous first performance of *The Seagull*, at the Alexandrinsky Theatre in St. Petersburg, 17 October.

1898   Begins association with the Moscow Art Theatre. Worsening tuberculosis forces him to move to Yalta. On 17 December, first successful performance of *The Seagull*, by the Moscow Art Theatre.

1899   First Moscow performance of *Uncle Vanya*, by the same company, 26 October. Publication begins of 'Collected Works', in ten volumes.

1901   First performance of *Three Sisters*, 31 January. Marries the Moscow Art Theatre actress Olga Knipper.

1903   Publishes last short story, *The Betrothed*.

1904   First performance of *The Cherry Orchard*, 17 January. Dies in Badenweiler, Germany, 2 July.

UNCLE VANYA

Scenes from country life in four acts

Dramatis Personae

SEREBRYAKOV, *Alexander Vladimirovich, a retired professor*
YELENA *Andreyevna, his wife, aged 27*
SONYA (*Sofya Alexandrovna*), *his daughter by his first marriage*
MARIA VASILIEVNA *Voinitskaya, widow of a Privy Councillor, mother of the professor's first wife*
VANYA, *Ivan Petrovich Voinitsky, her son*
ASTROV, *Mikhail Lvovich, a doctor*
TELEGIN, *Ilya Ilyich, an impoverished landowner*
MARINA, *an old nurse*
A WORKMAN

The action takes place on Serebryakov's country estate

For a Guide to Pronunciation of Names, see page 77

Act One

*A garden. Part of the house and a veranda can be seen. Under
an old poplar tree in the avenue, a table is set for tea. Benches
and chairs; on one of the benches lies a guitar, and a little way
off from the table is a swing. It is between two and three in the
afternoon, cloudy and overcast. MARINA, a stout, slow-
moving old woman, is sitting by the samovar, knitting a
stocking, and ASTROV is walking up and down nearby.*

MARINA (*pouring a glass of tea*). Have some tea, my dear.

ASTROV (*accepts it reluctantly*). I don't really feel like it.

MARINA. Maybe you'd take a drop of vodka?

ASTROV. No. No, I don't drink vodka every day.
Besides, it's rather close. (*A pause.*) Nanny, how long
have we known each other?

MARINA (*pondering*). How long? Goodness, let me think
. . . You came here, to these parts, when was it . . . ?
Sonya's mother, Vera Petrovna, was still alive. And you
were coming to us for two winters, while she was here
. . . so, that would make it about eleven years. (*After
some thought.*) Maybe more . . .

ASTROV. Have I changed much since then?

MARINA. Oh, a lot. You were young in those days, and

handsome, and now you've aged. You're not as good-
looking. And you like a drop of vodka now.

ASTROV. Yes . . . In ten years I've become a different
person. And what's the cause? Too much hard work,
Nanny. I'm on my feet the whole day, I don't know
the meaning of rest. I hide under the blanket at
night, afraid I'm going to be hauled out to see a
patient. In all the time we've known each other,
I haven't had a single day off. No wonder I've aged.
And life's boring in itself, mindless and squalid . . .
It drags you down, this life. You're surrounded by the
strangest people, cranks, all of them; you live amongst
them two or three years, and gradually, without even
noticing it, you become a crank yourself. It's inevitable.
(*Twirling his long moustache.*) And this huge moustache
I've grown . . . it's so stupid. Yes, I've become a crank,
Nanny . . . I haven't gone completely ga-ga yet, thank
God, my brain's still in one piece, but my feelings
have somehow got blunted. I don't want anything,
I don't need anything, I don't love anybody . . . Apart
from you, of course. (*Kisses her on the forehead.*) When
I was a child, I had a nanny just like you.

MARINA. Would you like something to eat?

ASTROV. No, thanks. In the third week of Lent, I had
to go to Malitskoye. There was an epidemic . . .
typhus . . . People stretched out in rows in the huts . . .
Filth, stench, smoke everywhere, calves lying on the
floor among the sick . . . young pigs too . . . I was on
the go all day, didn't sit down, not even a bite to eat,
and when I finally arrived home I got no rest either –

they brought in a signalman from the railway; I laid
him out on the table, and was about to operate, when
he upped and died on me, under the chloroform.
And just when I didn't need it, some sort of feeling
awoke in me, and my conscience started to nag at me,
as if I'd killed him deliberately . . . I sat down, closed
my eyes – like this, and started thinking: the people
who come after us, in two or three hundred years'
time, the people we're now clearing the way for – will
they remember us, d'you think? They won't, Marina,
will they.

MARINA. People won't remember, but God will.

ASTROV. Thank you. That was well said.

VANYA *enters, emerging from the house. He has had a nap
after lunch and looks a little dishevelled; he sits down on a
bench and fixes his fashionable tie.*

VANYA. Yes . . . (*A pause.*) Yes . . .

ASTROV. Had a good sleep?

VANYA. Yes . . . very. (*Yawns.*) You know, ever since the
Professor and his spouse came to stay, my life's been
out of joint . . . I sleep at the wrong time, eat all sorts
of spicy food at lunch and dinner, drink wine . . . it's
not healthy! We never used to have a spare minute,
Sonya and I worked non-stop – but now, Sonya does
all the work, and I do nothing but eat, drink and
sleep . . . It's unhealthy!

MARINA (*shaking her head*). Such goings-on! The
Professor doesn't get up till twelve, but the samovar's
kept boiling the whole morning, waiting for him.

Before they came we used to have dinner at one, same as everybody else, and now they're here it's at seven. The Professor reads and writes all night, and you'll suddenly hear the bell at about two . . . Heavens, what is it? Tea! So the servants have to be wakened, to put on the samovar . . . What a carry-on!

ASTROV. Will they be staying here much longer?

VANYA (*whistles*). A hundred years. The Professor's made up his mind to settle down.

MARINA. Look at this now. The samovar's been on the table the past two hours, and they've gone out for a walk.

VANYA. They're coming, they're coming . . . Don't worry.

Voices are heard off-stage. From the far end of the garden come SEREBRYAKOV, YELENA, SONYA *and* TELEGIN, *returning from their walk.*

SEREBRYAKOV. Splendid, absolutely splendid . . . The scenery's wonderful.

TELEGIN. Quite remarkable, Your Excellency.

SONYA. We'll go to the plantation tomorrow, papa – would you like that?

VANYA. Ladies and gentlemen – tea's ready!

SEREBRYAKOV. Dear friends, be so kind as to have tea sent up to my study. I've a few things still to do today.

SONYA. I'm sure you'll enjoy it at the plantation . . .

YELENA, SEREBRYAKOV *and* SONYA *exit into the house.* TELEGIN *goes over to the table and sits down beside* MARINA.

VANYA. It's stiflingly hot, yet our great scholar's wearing a coat and galoshes, and carrying his umbrella and gloves.

ASTROV. Taking good care of himself.

VANYA. And she's so lovely. So lovely! In my entire life, I've never seen a more beautiful woman.

TELEGIN (*to* MARINA). You know, dear lady, whether I'm riding through the fields, or walking in the shade in the garden, or just looking at this table, I experience a feeling of such bliss, I can't explain it! The weather's enchanting, the little birds are singing, we all live in peace and harmony here – what more could we ask? (*Accepts a glass of tea.*) Thank you most kindly!

VANYA (*dreamily*). Those eyes . . . A wonderful woman!

ASTROV. Tell us something, Vanya.

VANYA (*listlessly*). What've I got to tell you?

ASTROV. What, nothing new?

VANYA. No. All old stuff. I'm just the same as I was, except maybe worse, now that I've become lazy, and do nothing – apart from grumble, like some old fogey. And that old magpie of mine, my dear *maman*, still prattles on about the emancipation of women. She's got one eye fixed on her grave, while the other searches through her learned tomes, looking for the dawn of a new life.

ASTROV. And the Professor?

VANYA. The Professor, as ever, sits in his study from
morn till dead of night, writing. 'With anxious mind
and furrowed brow, we write and write and write, And
no praise ever comes our way, our labours to requite.'
I feel sorry for the paper! He'd do better to write his
autobiography. Now there's a superb subject! A retired
professor, you see, a dry old stick, a sort of scholarly
kipper . . . Gout, rheumatism, migraine, his liver
bloated with jealousy and envy . . . And this dried fish
lives on his first wife's estate, stays there against his
will, because he can't afford to live in town. He's
forever going on about his misfortunes, although in
point of fact he's been extraordinarily lucky.
(*Excitedly.*) Yes, just think, what luck he's had! The son
of a humble sacristan, he trains as a priest, somehow
manages to get university degrees and a professor-
ship, goes on to become 'Your Excellency', and the
son-in-law of a Senator, etc., etc. All that's neither
here nor there, but consider this. A man spends
twenty-five years, no less, lecturing and writing about
art, and doesn't understand the first thing about it.
For twenty-five years he's been chewing over other
people's ideas about realism, naturalism, and all
manner of nonsense; for twenty-five years he's been
lecturing and writing about things that any intelligent
person already knows, and no stupid person cares
to know. In a word, for twenty-five years he's been
pouring water into a sieve. And the self-importance of
the man! The pretensions! So now he's retired, and
nobody's ever heard of him, he's completely

unknown; which means that for twenty-five years he's been keeping somebody else out of a job. And look at him – strutting around, half-man, half-god!

ASTROV. Oh, come on, you envy him.

VANYA. Of course I envy him! Look at his success with women! No Don Juan ever experienced a more complete triumph! His first wife, my sister, a beautiful, gentle creature, as pure as that blue sky, a noble, generous woman, who had more admirers than he had students – she loved him the way only the angels can love beings as pure and beautiful as themselves. My mother, his mother-in-law, worships him to this day, and he still inspires her with a feeling of devout awe. His second wife, a beautiful, clever woman – you've just seen her – married him when he was already old, surrendered her youth, her beauty, her freedom, her radiance to him. What for? Why?

ASTROV. Is she faithful to the Professor?

VANYA. Unfortunately, yes.

ASTROV. What do you mean, unfortunately?

VANYA. Because that kind of faithfulness is a sham from beginning to end. It's got plenty of rhetoric, but no logic. To deceive an old husband, whom you can't abide – that's immoral; but to attempt to stifle your wretched youth, every living emotion you possess – that's not immoral?

TELEGIN (*tearfully*). Vanya, I don't like it when you say these things. It's the truth, you know . . . If somebody deceives their wife or husband, well, that means they're not to be trusted, they'd even betray their country!

VANYA (*irritated*). Oh, give it a rest, Waffles!

TELEGIN. Vanya, let me speak. My wife ran off with the man she loved, the day after our wedding, on account of my unprepossessing appearance. But I've never failed in my duty. I still love her, and I've stayed true to her. I help as much as I can, and I've given up everything I owned for her children's education, the ones she had by the man she loved. I've had to do without happiness, but I still have my pride. But what about her? She's lost her youth now, her beauty, in accordance with the laws of nature, has faded, and the man she loved is dead. What does she have left?

Enter SONYA *and* YELENA, *followed a moment later by* MARIA VASILIEVNA, *holding a book. She sits down and begins to read. A cup of tea is handed to her, and she drinks it without looking up.*

SONYA (*hurriedly, to* MARINA). Nanny dear, some peasants have come. Go and have a word with them, I'll look after the tea . . . (*Pours out the tea.*)

MARINA *exits*, YELENA *takes her cup of tea and drinks it sitting on the swing.*

ASTROV (*to* YELENA). I've actually come to see your husband. You wrote me that he was very ill, rheumatism and something else, but he seems perfectly fit.

YELENA. He was a bit depressed yesterday evening, complaining of pains in his legs, but he's all right today . . .

ASTROV. And I've galloped twenty miles at breakneck speed. Oh well, it's not the first time. I'll stay here overnight to make up for it – at least I'll be able to sleep *quantum satis*.

SONYA. That's wonderful. It's such a rare event, having you stay the night with us. You won't have had any dinner, I suppose?

ASTROV. No, I haven't.

SONYA. Then that's settled, you'll dine with us. We have dinner about seven these days. (*Drinks.*) This tea's cold!

TELEGIN. Yes, the temperature of the samovar has fallen significantly.

YELENA. Never mind, Ivan Ivanych, we can drink it cold.

TELEGIN. Forgive me, ma'am, but it's not Ivan Ivanych, it's Ilya Ilyich . . . Ilya Ilyich Telegin, or, as certain people call me on account of my pockmarked face – Waffles. I stood godfather at dear Sonya's christening, and His Excellency your husband knows me quite well. I live here now, ma'am, on this estate . . . If you've been kind enough to notice, I dine with you here every day.

SONYA. Mr Telegin helps us out – he's our right-hand man. (*Tenderly.*) Come on, godfather, I'll pour you another glass.

MARIA. Oh!

SONYA. What's the matter, grandma?

MARIA. I forgot to tell Alexander . . . my mind's going . . . I had a letter today from Pavel Alexeyevich in Kharkov . . . He's sent his new pamphlet.

ASTROV. Is it interesting?

MARIA. It is, but it's rather strange. He's now trying to disprove the very thing he was defending seven years ago. It's dreadful!

VANYA. There's nothing dreadful about it. Drink your tea, *maman*.

MARIA. But I want to talk!

VANYA. And we've been talking and reading pamphlets for fifty years now. It's time we called it a day.

MARIA. For some reason or other, you don't like listening when I talk. I'm sorry, *Jean*, but this past year you've changed so much I simply don't recognise you . . . You used to be a man of such firm convictions, a truly enlightened individual . . .

VANYA. Oh yes! I used to be an enlightened individual, only I never managed to enlighten anybody . . . (*A pause.*) An enlightened individual . . . you couldn't have come up with a more venomous jibe! I'm forty-seven years old now. And up until last year I made every effort, as did you, to blind myself with all this pedantic rubbish of yours, quite deliberately, to avoid seeing life as it really is – and I was doing rather well, I thought. But now – oh, if you only knew! I can't sleep at nights for sheer vexation, for resentment at having so stupidly wasted my time – that time when I might've had everything which my old age now denies me!

SONYA. Uncle Vanya, please, this is boring.

MARIA (*to her son*). It's almost as if you were accusing your former principles. But those aren't to blame, you are. You seem to have forgotten that principles are nothing in themselves, a dead letter . . . You should've been doing something.

VANYA. Doing something? It isn't everybody that can be a non-stop writing machine, like your Herr Professor.

MARIA. What's that supposed to mean?

SONYA (*imploringly*). Grandma! Uncle Vanya! Please!

VANYA. Right, right, I'll shut up. I'll shut up and apologise.

A pause.

YELENA. It's a lovely day. Not too hot . . .

A pause.

VANYA. A lovely day for hanging yourself . . .

TELEGIN *tunes his guitar.* MARINA *walks up and down near the house, calling the chickens.*

MARINA. Cheep, cheep, cheep . . .

SONYA. Nanny dear, what did those peasants want?

MARINA. Oh, same as usual, they're still after that bit of waste ground. Cheep, cheep, cheep . . .

SONYA. Which one are you calling?

MARINA. The speckled one, she's gone off somewhere with her chicks . . . Don't want the crows to
get them . . . (*Exits.*)

TELEGIN *plays a polka; everyone listens in silence. A*
WORKMAN *enters.*

WORKMAN. Is the doctor here? (*To* ASTROV.) Dr
Astrov, we've been sent to fetch you.

ASTROV. Sent from where?

WORKMAN. From the factory.

ASTROV (*irritated*). Thank you so much. Well, I suppose
I'd better go . . . (*Looks round for his cap.*) This is a
damned nuisance . . .

SONYA. It is annoying, really . . . Come back for dinner,
after the factory.

ASTROV. No, it'll be too late by then. No chance . . . (*To
the* WORKMAN.) Look, you might bring me a glass of
vodka, there's a good chap. (*The* WORKMAN *exits.*)
No, no hope, I'm afraid . . . (*Finds his cap.*) In one of
Ostrovsky's plays there's a character with a very large
moustache, and a very little talent . . . That's like me.
Anyway, I'll bid you goodbye . . . (*To* YELENA.) If you'd
like to drop in on me sometime, with Sonya here of
course, I'd be delighted. I have a small estate, ninety
acres or so, but if you're interested, there's a model
garden and nursery – you won't find their like for
hundreds of miles around. And there's a government
plantation alongside . . . The forester there's quite
old, and always ill, so I actually oversee all the work.

YELENA. Yes, you're very keen on trees, so I've been told. It's no doubt of great benefit, but doesn't it interfere with your real work? After all, you are a doctor.

ASTROV. Only God knows what our real work is.

YELENA. And is it interesting?

ASTROV. It is interesting, yes.

VANYA (*ironically*). Oh, very.

YELENA (*to* ASTROV). You're still young – you look about – what? Thirty-six, thirty-seven? It can't be that interesting, surely . . . Nothing but trees and more trees. I should think it was monotonous.

SONYA. No, it's extremely interesting. Dr Astrov plants new forests every year, and they've already sent him a bronze medal and a diploma. He goes to endless trouble to make sure the old forests aren't destroyed. And if you hear what he has to say, you'll agree with him absolutely. He says the forests beautify the earth, that they teach us to appreciate beauty, and instil a true majesty of spirit in us. Forests temper a harsh climate, and in countries with a mild climate, people spend less energy struggling with nature, so man himself is milder and more gentle. People in those countries are beautiful, pliant, easily moved, their speech is elegant, their gestures graceful. The arts and sciences flourish among them, their philosophy isn't gloomy, and their attitudes towards women are courteous and refined . . .

VANYA (*laughing*). Bravo, bravo! That's all very nice, but not convincing . . . (*To* ASTROV.) So, my friend, you won't mind if I carry on burning logs in my stove, and building my barns out of wood.

ASTROV. You can burn peat in your stove, and build your barns out of stone. Anyway, I don't mind people cutting wood from necessity, but why destroy the forests? Our Russian forests are groaning under the axe, millions of trees are perishing, the habitats of animals and birds are being laid waste, rivers are shrinking and drying up, the most wonderful landscapes are disappearing, never to return, all because some lazy individual hasn't the wit to bend down and pick up his firewood from the ground. (*To* YELENA.) Isn't it the truth, dear lady? A man would need to be a mindless savage to burn up such beauty in his stove, to destroy what he cannot create. We've been endowed with reason, and creative power, so we can increase what has been given to us, but up to now we've created nothing, only destroyed. There are fewer and fewer forests, the rivers are running dry, wild life is becoming extinct, the climate's ruined, and with each passing day the earth gets poorer and uglier. (*To* VANYA.) Yes, you're giving me that ironical look, you don't take anything I say seriously, and maybe . . . well, maybe I am a crank, but when I walk past the peasants' woods, which I've saved from being cut down, or when I hear my own young trees rustling, trees I've planted with my own hand, I'm conscious of the fact that the climate is in my control, to some extent, and that if people are happy a thousand years from now, then that will be my doing, to some extent, also. When I plant a birch tree, and see it coming into leaf, and swaying in the wind, my heart fills with pride, and I . . . (*Notices the* WORKMAN, *who has brought him a glass of vodka on a tray.*) Anyway . . . (*Drinks.*) It's time I was off. I suppose it's just one of my eccentricities, in the long run. Well, I bid you goodbye! (*Goes towards the house.*)

SONYA (*takes his arm and walks with him*). When will you come back to see us?

ASTROV. I don't know . . .

SONYA. In a month's time, again?

ASTROV *and* SONYA *exit to the house*; MARIA VASILIEVNA *and* TELEGIN *remain by the table*; YELENA *and* VANYA *walk towards the veranda.*

YELENA. Ivan Petrovich, you're impossible. Did you really need to annoy your mother, with all that talk about a writing machine? And you were arguing with Alexander at lunch again today. It's so petty!

VANYA. What if I hate the man?

YELENA. You've no reason to hate him, he's no different from anyone else. He's no worse than you.

VANYA. If you could just see your face, the way you move . . . As if everything's too much effort. Sheer indolence!

YELENA. Oh yes, indolent and bored. Everyone decries my husband, they all look at me with such compassion: poor, unhappy creature, she's got an old husband. Well, I know all about that kind of sympathy. It's just what Astrov was saying a moment ago: you destroy the forests without a thought, and soon there'll be nothing left on the earth. And you'd destroy a human being the same way, senselessly, and thanks to you, there'll soon be no fidelity, no integrity, no capacity for self-sacrifice left either! Why is it you can't look at a woman indifferently, unless she's yours? I'll tell you why – that doctor's right – it's because there's a demon of destruction in every one of you. You spare nothing, neither forests, nor birds, nor women, nor one another.

VANYA. I don't care for this line of thought!

A pause.

YELENA. The doctor has a tired, sensitive face. An interesting face. Sonya's obviously attracted to him; she's in love with him, and I can understand her feelings. He's been at the house three times since I've been here, but I'm too shy – I haven't once had a proper talk with him, or been nice to him. He'll think I'm bad-tempered. No doubt that's why we get on so well, Ivan Petrovich – that we're both such tiresome, boring people! Tiresome, yes! Don't look at me like that, please, I don't like it.

VANYA. How else can I look at you, if I love you? You're my happiness, my life, my youth! I know the chances of you returning my love are non-existent, virtually nil, but I don't want anything, just let me look at you, hear your voice . . .

YELENA. Sshh, they might hear you!

They walk towards the house.

VANYA (*following her*). Let me speak about my love,
    don't drive me away, and that'll be the greatest
    happiness for me . . .

YELENA. This is agony . . .

They exit into the house. TELEGIN *is strumming on his
guitar, playing a polka;* MARIA VASILIEVNA *is making
notes on the margins of her pamphlet.*

Curtain.

Act Two

The dining-room of the Serebryakov house. It is night, and the WATCHMAN *can be heard tapping in the garden.* SEREBRYAKOV *is sitting in an armchair in front of the open window, dozing.* YELENA *is sitting beside him, also dozing.*

SEREBRYAKOV (*waking up*). Who's that? Sonya, is that you?

YELENA. It's me.

SEREBRYAKOV. Oh, it's you, Lena . . . This pain, it's unbearable.

YELENA. Your rug's fallen on the floor. (*Wraps it around his legs.*) I'll close the window, Alexander.

SEREBRYAKOV. No, it's too stuffy. I dozed off just now, and dreamt my left leg didn't belong to me. Then I woke up with this agonizing pain. No, this isn't gout, it's more likely rheumatism. What time is it now?

YELENA. Twenty past twelve.

A pause.

SEREBRYAKOV. See if you can find Batyushkov in the library in the morning. I think we've got him.

YELENA. What?

SEREBRYAKOV. Batyushkov – have a look in the morning. We had a copy at one time, as I remember. Why am I finding it so hard to breathe?

YELENA. You're tired. This is your second night without sleep.

SEREBRYAKOV. They say Turgenev got angina from gout. I'm afraid I might do the same. Damnable, disgusting old age! To hell with it! Since I've grown old, I've become repellent even to myself. Yes, and all of you, no doubt, hate the sight of me.

YELENA. That tone of voice – you talk about your old age as if it was our fault.

SEREBRYAKOV. And you must hate me most of all.

YELENA *gets up and sits down a little way off.*

Well, you're right, of course. I'm not stupid, I do understand. You're a young woman, healthy, attractive, you want to live, and I'm an old man, practically a corpse. Isn't that so? D'you think I don't understand? And of course it's stupid of me to carry on living. Well, just wait a while, I'll set you all free soon enough. I haven't much longer to go.

YELENA. I'm worn out . . . For God's sake, be quiet.

SEREBRYAKOV. Yes, thanks to me, it seems, everybody's exhausted, bored, wasting their youth – I'm the only one who's contented, and enjoying life. Yes, of course.

YELENA. Oh, stop it! You're getting on my nerves.

SEREBRYAKOV. I get on everybody's nerves. Of course I do.

YELENA (*tearfully*). This is intolerable! What do you want from me, tell me!

SEREBRYAKOV. Nothing.

YELENA. Well, be quiet then. Please.

SEREBRYAKOV. You know, it's strange – when Ivan Petrovich starts talking, or his mother, that old fool, that's fine, everyone listens. But I've only to utter one word, and everyone starts feeling miserable. The very sound of my voice disgusts them. Well, supposing I am disgusting, selfish, a tyrant – surely I have a right to be selfish, in my old age? Haven't I earned it? I'm asking you, haven't I the right to a bit of peace, to a little consideration from people?

YELENA. Nobody's disputing your rights.

The window is banging in the wind.

The wind's getting up. I'll close the window. (*Does so.*) It's going to rain in a minute. No-one disputes your rights.

A pause. The WATCHMAN *is heard tapping in the garden, and singing a song.*

SEREBRYAKOV. You devote your entire life to learning, you grow accustomed to your study, to the lecture theatre, to your esteemed colleagues – and suddenly, for no discernible reason, you find yourself buried in this hole, looking at stupid people every day, listening to trivial chit-chat . . . I want to live, I love success, I enjoy being famous, causing a stir, and here – it's like being in exile. To spend every minute yearning for

what's past, watching other people succeed, fearing
death . . . I can't go on! I haven't the strength! And
then they can't forgive me for my old age!

YELENA. Wait a little while, have patience. In five or six
years, I'll be old too.

SONYA *enters.*

SONYA. Papa, you told us to send for Dr Astrov, and
now he's here you're refusing to see him. That isn't
nice. We've put him to a lot of trouble for nothing.

SEREBRYAKOV. What do I want with this Astrov of
yours? He knows as much about medicine as I know
about astronomy.

SONYA. Look, we can't summon the entire medical
faculty to attend to your gout.

SEREBRYAKOV. Well, I'm not going to talk to that
crank.

SONYA. Do as you please. (*Sits down.*) I don't care.

SEREBRYAKOV. What time is it now?

YELENA. It's after twelve.

SEREBRYAKOV. It's so stuffy. Sonya, hand me my drops
from the table.

SONYA. Right. (*Gives him the drops.*)

SEREBRYAKOV (*irritated*). No, not these! Oh, what's the
point of asking for anything!

SONYA. Don't make such a fuss, please. That might
work with some people, but not with me, if you don't

mind. I don't like it. And I haven't the time, I've an early rise tomorrow, we're cutting the hay.

VANYA enters in his dressing-gown, holding a candle.

VANYA. There's a storm on the way.

A flash of lightning.

There you are, you see? *Hélène* and Sonya, go to bed, I'll take over here.

SEREBRYAKOV (*alarmed*). No, no! Don't leave me with him! No! He'll talk me to death!

VANYA. But they need some peace! They haven't slept in two nights.

SEREBRYAKOV. Then let them go to bed, but you go too. Thanks all the same, but please go. For the sake of our former friendship, don't argue, please – we'll talk another time.

VANYA (*with a mocking smile*). Our former friendship . . . Former . . .

SONYA. Uncle Vanya, please . . .

SEREBRYAKOV (*to* YELENA). Don't leave me with him, my dear – he will, he'll talk me to death!

VANYA. This is getting ridiculous.

MARINA enters with a candle.

SONYA. You should be in bed, Nanny. It's late.

MARINA. The samovar hasn't been cleared away. I can't very well go to bed.

SEREBRYAKOV. Everybody's awake, everybody's worn out – except me, I'm blissfully happy.

MARINA (*goes up to* SEREBRYAKOV, *then soothingly*). What is it, my dear? Is it hurting again? My leg's hurting something awful too. (*Tucks his rug in.*) It's that old trouble of yours, that's what it is. Vera Petrovna, God rest her, Sonya's mother, she used to be up night after night with you, worried sick. She was so fond of you. (*A pause.*) Old folks are like children, they want people to feel sorry for them, but nobody pities us old folks, no. (*Kisses* SEREBRYAKOV *on the shoulder.*) Come on, my dear, let's go to bed . . . Come on, lovey . . . I'll make you some nice lime-flower tea, and warm your feet . . . And I'll say a prayer for you . . .

SEREBRYAKOV (*moved*). We'll go then, Marina.

MARINA. Yes, my leg's hurting something awful, it is. (*She and* SONYA *lead him out.*) Yes, Vera Petrovna used to be worried sick, crying all the time. You were just a girl then, Sonya love, a silly little thing. Now, off we go, my dear . . .

SEREBRYAKOV, SONYA *and* MARINA *exit.*

YELENA. I'm worn out with him. I can hardly stand.

VANYA. You're worn out with him, I'm worn out with myself. I haven't slept in three nights.

YELENA. There's something seriously amiss in this house. Your mother hates everything except those pamphlets of hers and the Professor; the Professor's constantly irritated, he doesn't trust me, and he's afraid of you. Sonya's annoyed with her father, and annoyed with me – she hasn't spoken to me for two weeks now. You detest my husband, and openly despise your own mother. And I'm upset – I've been on the verge of tears a dozen times already today. No, there's something badly amiss in this house.

VANYA. We can do without the philosophy.

YELENA. You're an educated man, Vanya, a clever man – you surely ought to know that it's not fire and gangs of thieves destroying the world, but hatred, enmity, all these petty squabbles . . . You should be trying to keep the peace, not complaining all the time.

VANYA. Then first make me at peace with myself! Oh, my darling . . . (*Suddenly bends down to kiss her hand.*)

YELENA. Stop it! (*Pulls her hand free.*) Go away!

VANYA. The rain'll be over in a minute, and everything in nature'll be refreshed, breathing easily again. Except me, the storm won't refresh me. Day and night, it's like some sort of hobgoblin, choking me, the thought that my life's wasted, gone beyond recall. I've no past, it's been stupidly squandered on trifles, and my present is so absurd it's terrifying. So there you have it, my life and love: where am I to put them, what's to be done with them? My feelings for you are dying to no purpose, like a ray of sunlight falling into a pit, and I'm dying along with them.

YELENA. When you talk to me about your love, I just go numb, and I don't know what to say. I'm sorry, there's nothing I can tell you. (*Makes to leave.*) Good night.

VANYA (*barring her way*). And if you only knew how much I suffer, knowing that there's another life perishing alongside mine in this house – yours! What are you waiting for? What damned philosophy's holding you back? Think, for God's sake, think!

YELENA (*looks at him intently*). Ivan Petrovich, you're drunk.

VANYA. Possibly. It's possible . . .

YELENA. Where's the doctor?

VANYA. He's in there . . . In my room, he's staying the night. Yes, it's possible. Anything's possible.

YELENA. And you've been drinking today? What on earth for?

VANYA. At least it's some sort of life . . . *Hélène*, don't make me stop.

YELENA. You never used to drink. And you never used to talk so much . . . Go to bed. You're getting on my nerves.

VANYA (*impulsively kissing her hand*). Oh, my darling . . . wonderful . . .

YELENA (*angrily*). Stop it! Leave me alone! This is disgusting. Honestly! (*Exits.*)

VANYA (*alone*). She's gone . . . (*A pause.*) I first met her at my sister's house, ten years ago. She was seventeen, and I was thirty-seven. Why didn't I fall in love with her then, and ask her to marry me? It would've been quite possible. And she would be my wife now . . .

Yes . . . We'd both have been wakened by the storm just now; she'd be frightened by the thunder, I'd hold her in my arms and whisper: 'Don't be afraid, I'm here.' Oh, it's a wonderful thought, so beautiful, it actually makes me laugh . . . but, dear God, my mind's in such a muddle . . . Why am I old? Why doesn't she understand me? That empty rhetoric of hers, that facile morality – her silly, half-baked ideas about the destruction of the world – I detest all that. (*A pause.*) Oh, I've been cheated so badly! I worshipped that Professor, that sorry gout-ridden specimen, I worked like a slave for him! Sonya and I squeezed every last drop out of this estate; we sold linseed oil, and peas, and curds, haggling like peasants, skimping on food, saving up every miserable kopeck so we could send him thousands of roubles! I was so proud of him and his learning, I lived and breathed for that man! Everything he wrote, every word he uttered, seemed to me like a work of genius . . . And now? My God . . . Here he is, retired, and the sum total of his life is plain to see. Not one page of his labours will survive him, he's completely unknown, a nonentity! A soap bubble! And I've been cheated . . . I can see it now – stupidly deceived . . .

ASTROV *enters wearing a coat, but no waistcoat or tie; he is slightly drunk. He is followed by* TELEGIN, *with his guitar.*

ASTROV. Play!

TELEGIN. They're all asleep.

ASTROV. Go on, play!

TELEGIN *begins quietly strumming.*

ASTROV (*to* VANYA). All alone here? No ladies? (*Stands with his arms akimbo, begins quietly singing.*) 'Go, little hut, go, little stove too – now what will poor master do? . . . ' The storm woke me up. Fair old spot of rain. What time is it?

VANYA. God knows.

ASTROV. I thought I heard Yelena Andreyevna's voice.

VANYA. She was here a moment ago.

ASTROV. A glorious woman. (*Inspects the medicine bottles on the table.*) Medicines. Prescriptions from all over the place . . . Kharkov, Moscow, Tula . . . He's plagued every town in Russia with his gout. Is he ill, or just pretending?

VANYA. He's ill.

A pause.

ASTROV. Why are you so glum today? Feeling sorry for the Professor, is that it?

VANYA. Leave me alone.

ASTROV. Or maybe you're in love with the Professor's wife?

VANYA. She's my friend.

ASTROV. Already?

VANYA. What's that mean – 'already'?

ASTROV. Well, a woman can only become a man's friend in a certain sequence: first, charming acquaintance, then mistress, then friend.

VANYA. That's a rather crude outlook.

ASTROV. Really? Yes . . . I have to admit – I am becoming rather crude. See, I'm even drunk. As a rule, I get this drunk only once a month. When I'm in this state I become arrogant and insolent in the extreme. I don't give a damn about anything. I take on the most difficult operations and do them beautifully; I draw up the most ambitious plans for the future. At times like this I no longer see myself as a crank – I believe I'm of tremendous benefit to mankind – tremendous! At such times I have my own personal philosophical system, and all of you, my friends, appear to me like insects . . . or microbes. (*To* TELEGIN.) Waffles, play!

TELEGIN. Dearest good friend, I'd be happy to, with all my heart, but do remember – people are asleep.

ASTROV. Play, I said! (TELEGIN *begins softly playing.*) I could do with a drink. Come on, I think there's still some cognac left. As soon as it's light we'll go to my place. Roight? I've got a male nurse who never says 'right', but 'roight'. A terrible rogue. All roight, then? (*Catches sight of* SONYA *entering.*) I beg your pardon – I'm not dressed . . . (*Hurriedly exits.* TELEGIN *follows him out.*)

SONYA. Uncle Vanya, you've been drinking with the doctor again. You're a fine pair! He's always like that, but why you? It's not very becoming at your age.

VANYA. Age has nothing to do with it. When people have no real life, they live off illusions. They're better than nothing.

SONYA. The hay's all been cut, and it's raining every day – everything's rotting, and you sit daydreaming. You've completely neglected the estate . . . I've had to work on my own, and I'm absolutely worn out . . . (*Alarmed.*) Uncle, you have tears in your eyes!

VANYA. What tears? Nothing of the kind . . . non-sense . . . The way you looked at me then – just like your mother. Oh, dearest Sonya . . . (*Feverishly kisses her hands and face.*) My sister . . . my darling sister . . . where is she now? If only she knew! Oh, if only she knew!

SONYA. Knew what? Uncle, if she knew what?

VANYA. It's too painful . . . I feel terrible . . . No, it doesn't matter . . . Later . . . It's nothing . . . I'll go . . . (*Exits.*)

SONYA (*knocks at* ASTROV'S *door*). Doctor? You're not asleep, are you? A minute, please.

ASTROV (*behind the door*). Just coming! (*Enters a few moments later. He is now wearing his waistcoat and tie.*) What can I do for you?

SONYA. Doctor, you can drink if you want, if it doesn't bother you, but please don't let my uncle drink. It's not good for him.

ASTROV. Fine. We won't drink any more (*A pause.*) I'm leaving for home now. Signed, sealed and delivered. By the time the horses are ready it'll be daylight.

SONYA. It's still raining. Wait till morning.

ASTROV. The storm's passing us by, we'll just catch the edge of it. I'll go now. And please, don't ask me to attend your father again. I tell him he has gout, he tells me it's rheumatism; I ask him to go to bed, he stays up. And today he wouldn't even speak to me.

SONYA. He's been spoiled. (*Goes over to the sideboard.*) Would you like something to eat?

ASTROV. Yes, why not?

SONYA. I like a snack at night-time. I think there's something in the sideboard. You know, he's supposed to have been a big success with women in his day, and the ladies have spoiled him. Here, have some cheese.

They both stand by the sideboard and eat.

ASTROV. I haven't had a thing to eat today, just drink. Your father's a difficult man. (*Takes a bottle out of the sideboard.*) May I? (*Drinks a glass.*) There's no-one else here, and I can speak frankly. You know, I don't think I could survive a month in this house, I'd simply suffocate in this atmosphere . . . Your father, going on all the time about his gout, and his books, Uncle Vanya, with his depression, that grandmother of yours, and on top of that, your stepmother . . .

SONYA. What about my stepmother?

ASTROV. Everything about a human being should be beautiful – face, clothes, soul, thoughts. And she is beautiful, there's no denying it, but . . . I mean, all she does is eat, sleep, go for walks, enchant us all with her beauty, and that's it. She has no responsibilities, other people work for her . . . Isn't that the case? And an idle life can't be virtuous. (*A pause.*) Well, maybe I'm being too severe. I'm dissatisfied with life, like your Uncle Vanya, and we're becoming a pair of old grumblers.

SONYA. Are you really not content with life?

ASTROV. I actually love life, but this narrow, provincial Russian life of ours I simply can't abide, I despise it with every fibre of my being. And as for my own personal life, God knows, I can find absolutely nothing good in it. You know, if you're walking through the forest on a dark night, and you happen to see a light shining in the distance, you don't notice your fatigue, or the dark, or the thorny branches, whipping against your face . . . I work, as you well know, harder than anyone else in this province, I suffer the blows of fate incessantly, at times it's unbearable, but I don't have any light shining in the distance. I no longer expect anything for myself, I really don't like people . . . I haven't cared for anybody in years.

SONYA. Nobody?

ASTROV. No. I feel a certain affection towards your old nurse, that's all – for old time's sake. The peasants are all alike, backward, living in squalor, and I can't get along with our intelligentsia – it's hard work, they wear you out. The whole lot of them, all our good friends, they're so shallow, the way they think and feel, they can't see farther than the end of their

noses – to put it bluntly, they're stupid. And those
with a bit more intelligence and substance to them
are hysterical, consumed with analysis and intro-
spection . . . They do nothing but whine, indulging
their petty hatreds and morbid slanders; they sidle up
to a man and squint at him out of the corner of their
eyes, and deliver their judgment: 'Yes, that one's a
neurotic!' or, 'Oh, he's full of hot air!' And since they
don't know what label to stick on my forehead, they
say, 'He's a strange man, very strange.' I love the
forest – that's strange; I don't eat meat, that's strange
too. No, there's no longer any spontaneous, pure, free
relationship with nature, or with other people . . .
Absolutely none! (*He is about to drink.*)

SONYA (*prevents him.*) No, please don't . . . don't drink
any more.

ASTROV. Why not?

SONYA. It's just so unlike you. You're so refined, you
have such a gentle voice . . . Besides, more than
anyone else I know, you're a wonderful person. So
why do you want to be like these commonplace
people, the kind of men who drink and play cards?
No no, please don't do that. You always say people
don't create, they only destroy what's been given to
them from on high. Well, then, why are you
destroying yourself? Please, please, you mustn't, I
implore you!

ASTROV (*holds out his hand to her.*) I won't drink any
more.

SONYA. Give me your word.

ASTROV. Word of honour.

SONYA (*warmly squeezes his hand*). Thank you.

ASTROV. Enough! I've sobered up. You can see I'm
sober now, and I'll stay like that till the end of my
days. (*Looks at his watch.*) Anyway, to continue . . . As
I was saying, my time's past, it's too late for me . . .
I've grown old, I'm burned out, I've become coarse
and vulgar, my emotions are dulled, and I don't think
I could become attached to anyone. I don't love
anyone, and now I never will. What still attracts me is
beauty. I'm not indifferent to that. And frankly, if
Yelena Andreyevna wanted to, she could turn my head
in a single day . . . However, that's not love, that's not
affection . . . (*Covers his eyes with his hand and shudders.*)

SONYA. What's the matter?

ASTROV. Nothing . . . Just before Easter, one of my
patients died under the chloroform.

SONYA. It's time you forgot about that. (*A pause.*)
Doctor, tell me something . . . Say I had a girlfriend,
or a younger sister, and you found out that she . . .
well, let's say she was in love with you, how would you
feel about that?

ASTROV (*shrugs*). I don't know. I'd probably feel
nothing at all. I'd let her know I couldn't love her . . .
and besides, I've got other things on my mind.
Anyway, I'd better go, if I'm going. I'll say goodbye,
my dear, or it'll be morning before we're finished.
(*Presses her hand.*) I'll go out through the drawing-

room, if I may, otherwise I'm afraid your uncle might detain me. (*Exits.*)

SONYA (*alone*). He didn't tell me anything . . . His heart and soul are still hidden from me, yet why do I feel so happy? (*Laughs from sheer joy.*) I said to him: you're so refined, so noble, you have such a gentle voice . . . did that sound out of place? His voice thrills me, it's so caressing . . . I feel it in the air even now. But when I spoke to him about a younger sister, he didn't understand . . . (*Wringing her hands.*) Oh, it's dreadful that I'm so plain! It's terrible! I know I'm not attractive, I know it, I know it . . . Last Sunday, when we were coming out of church, I heard them talking about me, and one woman said: 'She's such a kind girl, so goodhearted, it's just a pity she's so plain . . . ' So plain . . .

YELENA *enters*.

YELENA (*opens the windows*). The storm's over. What lovely fresh air! (*A pause.*) Where's the doctor?

SONYA. He's gone.

A pause.

YELENA. Sophie . . .

SONYA. Yes?

YELENA. How long are you going to stay cross with me? We haven't done each other any harm. Why should we be enemies? Let's call it a day.

SONYA. I've been wanting to . . . (*Embraces her.*) No more anger.

YELENA. Excellent!

They are both very excited.

SONYA. Has papa gone to bed?

YELENA. No, he's sitting in the drawing-room. We don't talk to each other for weeks on end, God knows why . . . (*She notices the sideboard is open.*) What's this?

SONYA. The doctor was having some supper.

YELENA. And there's wine . . . Let's drink to our friendship.

SONYA. Yes, let's.

YELENA. Out of the same glass . . . (*Fills it.*) It's better that way. So . . . we're friends now?

SONYA. Friends. (*They drink, and kiss.*) I've been wanting to make it up with you for ages, but I felt ashamed somehow. (*Begins to cry.*)

YELENA. Heavens, what are you crying for?

SONYA. It's nothing, I can't help it.

YELENA. There, there . . . (*Begins to cry.*) Silly, I'm crying too, now . . . (*A pause.*) You're angry with me because you think I married your father for money. If you believe in oaths, then I'll swear to you I married him for love. I was attracted to him as a famous learned man. It wasn't genuine love, it was artificial, but it seemed real enough to me at the time. I'm not to blame. But from the very day of our wedding you've never stopped punishing me with those clever, suspicious eyes of yours.

SONYA. Anyway, peace, peace! Let's forget all that.

YELENA. You shouldn't look at people like that – it doesn't become you. You should trust people – otherwise life's just impossible.

A pause.

SONYA. Tell me truthfully, as a friend . . . Are you happy?

YELENA. No.

SONYA. I knew that. One more question. Tell me honestly – wouldn't you have liked a young husband?

YELENA. What a child you are still. Of course I would. (*Laughs.*) Well, ask me something else – go on . . .

SONYA. Do you like the doctor?

YELENA. Yes, very much.

SONYA (*laughs*). I look silly, don't I? I mean, he's gone now, but I can still hear his voice and his footsteps, and when I look at the dark window, it's as if I can see his face there. Let me tell you about it . . . But I can't say it out loud, I'm too ashamed. Let's go to my room, we can talk there. Do I seem silly to you? Now, confess . . . Tell me something about him . . .

YELENA. What d'you mean?

SONYA. He's so clever . . . He knows how to do things, he can do anything . . . He heals the sick, and he plants forests . . .

YELENA. It's not a question of medicine or forests . . . My dear, don't you understand? He has genius! And

you know what that means? It means boldness,
freedom of mind, breadth of vision . . . He plants a
little tree, and already he's wondering what will come
of it in a thousand years' time, he's already dreaming
of the happiness of mankind. People like him are so
rare, we must love them . . . Yes, he drinks, he's
sometimes rather coarse, but what does that matter?
No man of genius in Russia can be entirely without
fault. Just imagine the sort of life that doctor leads!
Impassable muddy roads, freezing cold, blizzards,
enormous distances, an uncouth, primitive people,
poverty and disease all around him – I mean, in
conditions like that, slaving away day in, day out, it
would be hard for any man to keep himself chaste
and sober until he was forty . . . (*Kisses her.*) I wish you
happiness with all my heart, you deserve it . . . (*Stands
up.*) Anyway, I'm a tiresome creature, a person of no
importance. In my music, in my husband's house, in
all my little romantic affairs – everywhere, in fact, I've
never been of any consequence. Actually, Sonya, when
you come to think of it, I'm a very, very unfortunate
woman. (*She is pacing about the stage in agitation.*)
There's no happiness for me on this earth – none!
Why are you laughing?

SONYA (*laughs, covering her face*). I'm just so happy . . .
so happy!

YELENA. I feel like playing the piano . . . I could play
something just now.

SONYA. Do, please. (*Embraces her.*) I can't sleep . . . Play
something.

YELENA. In a minute. Your father isn't asleep. Music irritates him when he's sick. Go and ask him. If he doesn't mind, I'll play. On you go.

SONYA. Right. (*Exits.*)

The WATCHMAN *is heard tapping in the garden.*

YELENA. It's been ages since I've played. I'll play and I'll cry . . . cry like a silly girl. (*Calls out of the window.*) Yefim, is that you knocking?

WATCHMAN (*off-stage*). It's me!

YELENA. Don't do that, the master's not well.

WATCHMAN. I'm just going! (*Whistles to his dog.*) Come on, Blackie! Good boy! Blackie, come on!

A pause.

SONYA (*returning*). We can't!

Curtain.

Act Three

The drawing-room of SEREBRYAKOV's *house. Three doors,
at right, left and centre. Afternoon.* VANYA *and* SONYA
are seated, while YELENA *paces about the stage, deep in
thought.*

VANYA. The Herr Professor has graciously expressed the
desire that we should all assemble here in this
drawing-room today at one o'clock. (*Looks at his
watch.*) Quarter to one. He wishes to make some
statement to the world.

YELENA. Probably a business matter.

VANYA. He hasn't any sort of business. All he does is
write nonsense, grumble, and feel jealous.

SONYA (*reproachfully*). Uncle!

VANYA. All right, all right, I'm sorry. (*Points at*
YELENA.) Just look at her. Practically staggering
from sheer indolence. Charming. Quite charming.

YELENA. And you keep droning on the whole day, on
and on. Don't you ever get fed up? (*Wistfully.*) I'm
dying of boredom, I just don't know what to do.

SONYA (*shrugs*). Well, there's plenty to do. If you felt like
it . . .

YELENA. Like what, for instance?

SONYA. You could help with running the estate, teach
children, or look after the sick. That's plenty, surely?
And before you and papa came, Uncle Vanya and I
used to go to the market ourselves and sell the flour.

YELENA. I wouldn't know how. And besides, it's not
very interesting. It's only in romantic novels that
people teach school and nurse the peasants. How am
I going to take up teaching and nursing all of a
sudden, just out of the blue?

SONYA. Well, that's what I don't understand. How can
you help not going out to teach? Anyway, wait a while,
and you'll get used to the idea. (*Embraces her.*) Try not
to be bored, my dearest. (*Laughs.*) You're bored, you
don't know what to do with yourself, but boredom and
idleness are infectious. Look – Uncle Vanya does
nothing, all he does is follow you around like a
shadow, while I've left my work and come running
in to have a chat with you. I've grown lazy, I can't
help it! Doctor Astrov used to visit us only very rarely,
once a month perhaps, and he took some persuading,
but now he rides over here every day – he's aban-
doned his forests and medicine both. You must be
a witch.

VANYA. What are you pining away for? (*Animatedly.*)
Come on, my dearest, you glorious creature, be
sensible! You've got mermaid's blood flowing in your
veins, be a mermaid! Let yourself go even just once in
your life, fall madly in love with some water-sprite,
and plunge headlong into the depths – make the

Herr Professor and all of us throw up our hands in horror!

YELENA (*angrily*). Leave me alone! This is so cruel! (*Makes to exit.*)

VANYA (*prevents her*). No, please, please, my darling, forgive me . . . I'm truly sorry. (*Kisses her hand.*) Peace?

YELENA. You'd try the patience of a saint, honestly.

VANYA. As a token of peace and harmony I'll bring you a bouquet of roses; I've had them ready for you since morning . . . Autumn roses – beautiful, melancholy roses . . . (*Exits.*)

SONYA. Autumn roses – beautiful, melancholy roses.

Both women look out of the window.

YELENA. It's September already. How are we going to get through the winter here? (*A pause.*) Where's the doctor?

SONYA. He's in Uncle Vanya's room. Writing something. I'm glad Uncle Vanya's gone out, I need to have a talk with you.

YELENA. What about?

SONYA. What about? (*Lays her head against* YELENA's *bosom.*)

YELENA. There, there . . . (*Strokes her hair.*) It's all right . . .

SONYA. I'm not attractive.

YELENA. You have beautiful hair.

SONYA. No! (*Turns round to look at herself in the mirror.*)
No! When a woman isn't attractive, they always say:
'You have beautiful eyes, you have beautiful hair' . . .
I've loved him now for six years, I love him more than
my own mother. I seem to hear him every minute, I
can feel the pressure of his hand, and I watch the
door, waiting, thinking he's just about to enter. And
you see how I keep coming to you, to talk about him.
He's here every day now, but he doesn't look at me,
he doesn't see me . . . It's sheer torture! I've no hope
at all, absolutely none! (*In despair.*) Oh God, give me
strength . . . I've been praying the whole night . . . I
often go up to him, start talking to him, look into his
eyes . . . I've no pride left, I can't control myself . . . I
just couldn't help it, yesterday I told Uncle Vanya I
was in love . . . And all the servants know I love him.
Everybody knows.

YELENA. And what about him?

SONYA. He doesn't even notice me.

YELENA (*musing*). He's a strange man . . . I'll tell you
what – why don't I have a word with him? I'll be very
careful, do it in a roundabout way . . . (*A pause.*) I
mean, really, to go all this time without knowing . . .
Let me try. (SONYA *nods her consent.*) Splendid. He
either loves you or he doesn't – that won't be difficult
to find out. Don't be embarrassed, my darling, and
don't worry – I'll question him very tactfully, he won't
even be aware. Yes or no, that's all we need to know.
(*A pause.*) If it's no, then perhaps he shouldn't come
here any more. Right? (SONYA *nods.*) It'll be easier if

you're not seeing him. We won't put it off, we'll speak
to him right now. He was going to show me some of
his charts . . . Go and tell him I'd like to see him.

SONYA (*greatly agitated*). You'll tell me the truth?

YELENA. Yes, of course. I think the truth, no matter
what, can't be more terrible than not knowing. You
can trust me, my darling.

SONYA. Yes . . . yes . . . I'll tell him you want to see his
charts . . . (*Goes to the door and stops.*) No, it's better not
knowing . . . At least there's hope . . .

YELENA. What did you say?

SONYA. Nothing. (*Exits.*)

YELENA (*alone*). There's nothing worse than knowing
somebody else's secret, and not being able to help.
(*Musing.*) He's not in love with her, that's obvious, but
why shouldn't he marry her? She's not attractive, but
for a country doctor, someone of his age, she'd make
an excellent wife. Intelligent, extremely kind,
innocent . . . No, that's not the point . . . (*A pause.*)
I understand that poor girl. In the midst of this
desperate boredom, surrounded by grey shadows
wandering in and out, instead of human beings,
listening to vulgar chit-chat from people who know
nothing but eating, drinking and sleeping – now and
again he appears, so different from the rest, handsome, interesting, attractive, like a bright moon rising
in the darkness . . . To fall under the spell of such a
man, to forget oneself . . . I think I'm a little in love
myself. Yes, I'm bored when he's not here, and just

look at me, smiling when I think of him. Uncle Vanya says I have mermaid's blood in my veins. 'Let yourself go even just once in your life' . . . Well? Perhaps that's what I should do . . . Just fly away, free as a bird, away from all of you, away from your sleepy faces, and your talk, just forget you even exist . . . But I'm too cowardly, too timid . . . My conscience would torment me . . . Yet he comes here every day, I can guess why, and I already feel guilty . . . I feel like kneeling before Sonya and begging her forgiveness, crying . . .

ASTROV (*enters carrying a chart*). Good afternoon. (*They shake hands.*) You wanted to see my painting?

YELENA. You promised yesterday you'd show me your work. Have you the time?

ASTROV. But of course! (*Spreads the chart on a card-table and fixes it with drawing-pins.*) Where were you born?

YELENA (*helping him.*) In Petersburg.

ASTROV. And where did you study?

YELENA. At the music conservatory.

ASTROV. I don't suppose this'll interest you.

YELENA. Why not? I don't know much about the country, it's true, but I've read a good deal.

ASTROV. I have my own work-table here . . . In Vanya's room. When I'm absolutely worn out, to the point of stupefaction, I drop everything and escape here, amuse myself with this stuff for an hour or two . . . Vanya and Sonya click away at their abacus, doing the accounts, and I sit alongside them at my own table, messing about with my paints – it's warm, and quiet, and the cricket chirps. However, that's a pleasure I allow myself only rarely, once a month . . . (*Pointing to the chart.*) Look at this now. This is a map of our district as it was fifty years ago. The dark and light green represent forest; half of the entire area was covered with woodland. Where the green's cross-hatched with red, that used to be inhabited by elks and wild goats . . . I show both flora and fauna on this. This lake was home to swans, geese, ducks – as the old folks say, a 'power of birds' of all sorts, no end of them: they used to fly in great clouds. Apart from the villages and hamlets, you can see scattered here and there various little settlements – small farms, Old Believers' hermitages, water-mills . . . There were a lot of cattle and horses too. That's shown in blue. In this district, for example, the blue's very heavy; there were droves of horses here, an average of three to every homestead. (*A pause.*) Now let's look lower down. This is how it was twenty-five years ago. Already there's only a third of the total area given over to forest. The wild goats have gone, but there are still some elks. The green and blue colours are paler. And so on, and so forth. Now we turn to the third section, showing the district as it is now. The green appears here and there, but only in patches, not solid; the elks have disappeared, so have the swans, and grouse . . . And there's no trace of the earlier settlements, the farms, hermitages, mills. In general it's a picture of gradual and unmistakable decay, which will quite clearly be complete, in another ten to fifteen years. You may say there are cultural influences at work, that the old way of life must naturally give way to the new. Well, yes, I can understand that, if these devastated forests had been replaced by good roads and railways, if we now had workshops, factories, schools – the people would be better off, healthier, more intelligent, but there's clearly nothing of the kind! We still have the same swamps and mosquitoes, the same trackless waste, the same poverty, typhus, diphtheria, fires . . . What we're dealing with here is a case of degeneration, the outcome of a back-breaking struggle for existence – a degeneration caused by inertia, by ignorance, by a complete lack of self-awareness, as when a sick man, starving, chilled to the bone, in order to save what's left of his life, to protect his children, will instinctively, unconsciously, grab hold of anything that might satisfy his hunger or warm him, and in so doing destroy everything, without a thought for tomorrow . . . We've already destroyed almost everything, and created nothing yet to take its place. (*Coldly.*) I can see by your expression that this doesn't interest you.

YELENA. But I understand so little of these things . . .

ASTROV. There's nothing to understand, you're just not interested.

YELENA. To tell you the truth, my mind was elsewhere. I'm sorry. Actually, I want to put you through a little interrogation, and I'm embarrassed. I don't know how to begin.

ASTROV. An interrogation?

YELENA. Yes, an interrogation, but . . . well, it's quite innocent. Let's sit down. (*They sit.*) It's to do with a certain young person. We'll talk openly, as friends, without beating about the bush. We'll have a little talk, then forget all about it. Yes?

ASTROV. Yes.

YELENA. It concerns my stepdaughter Sonya. Tell me, do you like her?

ASTROV. Yes, I respect her.

YELENA. Do you like her as a woman?

ASTROV (*after a pause*). No.

YELENA. Another few words, and that'll be the end. You haven't noticed anything?

ASTROV. No, nothing.

YELENA (*takes his hand*). You don't love her, I can see it in your eyes . . . She's suffering . . . You must realise that, and . . . stop coming here.

ASTROV (*stands up*). I've outstayed my welcome. Anyway, I've no time . . . (*Shrugs.*) When do I ever have time? (*He is embarrassed.*)

YELENA. Whew, what an unpleasant conversation! I'm all on edge, as if I've been carrying a ton weight around. Well, that's that over, thank God. We'll forget this, as if we'd never mentioned it, and . . . and you can leave now. You're an intelligent man, you do understand . . . (*A pause.*) I feel quite flushed.

ASTROV. If you'd told me this a month or two ago,
I might've taken it seriously, but now . . . (*Shrugs.*)
Of course, if she's suffering, well . . . Just one thing
I don't understand: why did you need to have this
interrogation? (*Looks into her eyes, and wags his finger
accusingly.*) Oh, you're a crafty one!

YELENA. What's that supposed to mean?

ASTROV (*laughing*). So clever! All right, let's say Sonya
is suffering, I can readily accept that, but what's the
point of this interrogation of yours? (*Prevents her from
speaking, animatedly.*) Oh, please, don't look so
surprised, you know perfectly well why I come here
every day . . . Why, and on whose account – you
know very well indeed. And don't look at me like
that, you charming predatory creature – I'm too wise
a bird . . .

YELENA (*bewildered*). Predatory? I don't understand.

ASTROV. A beautiful, fluffy little weasel . . . And you
need a victim! I've spent an entire month doing
nothing, I've dropped everything to chase after you –
and that pleases you enormously, oh yes! Well, what
now? I'm conquered, you knew that even without an
interrogation. (*Folds his arms and hangs his head.*)
I submit. Here I am, devour me!

YELENA. You've gone mad!

ASTROV (*laughs sardonically*). You're shy . . .

YELENA. Oh, I'm not as bad as you think, I'm not so
low! I swear to you! (*Makes to exit.*)

ASTROV (*barring her way*). I'm leaving today, I won't be back again, but . . . (*Takes her by the hand, and looks round.*) Where shall we meet? Tell me, quickly – where? Someone might come in – tell me, quickly. (*Passionately.*) You're so wonderful, glorious . . . Just one kiss . . . Let me kiss your beautiful, fragrant hair . . .

YELENA. I swear to you . . .

ASTROV (*prevents her from speaking*). Why swear anything? There's no need to swear. No need for words . . . oh, you're so beautiful! Such lovely hands! (*Kisses her hands.*)

YELENA. No, please, stop it . . . go away . . . (*Withdraws her hands.*) You're forgetting yourself.

ASTROV. Then tell me, tell me! Where shall we meet tomorrow? (*Puts his arms round her waist.*) It's inevitable, don't you see? We must meet. (*He kisses her. At that same moment* VANYA *enters with a bouquet of roses and stops in the doorway.*)

YELENA (*not seeing* VANYA). Have pity on me, please . . . leave me alone . . . (*Lays her head on* ASTROV's *chest.*) No! (*Tries to go.*)

ASTROV (*holding her by the waist*). Come to the plantation tomorrow . . . at two o'clock . . . Yes? Yes? You'll come?

YELENA (*catching sight of* VANYA). Let me go! (*Acutely embarrassed, goes over to the window.*) This is terrible.

VANYA (*lays the bouquet down on a chair; nervously wipes his face and neck with his handkerchief*). It's all right . . . Yes . . . It's all right . . .

ASTROV (*unabashed*). The weather's not bad today, my dear Ivan Petrovich. Overcast in the morning, looked like rain, but now it's sunny. One must say, autumn's turned out splendidly . . . and the winter crops are coming along. (*Rolls up his chart.*) Only thing is – the days are getting shorter . . . (*Exits.*)

YELENA (*quickly goes up to* VANYA). You must try, you must use all your influence to see that my husband and I leave here this very day! Do you hear? This very day!

VANYA (*mopping his brow*). Eh? Oh, yes . . . fine . . . I saw everything, *Hélène*, everything . . .

YELENA (*agitatedly*). Do you hear? I've got to get away from this place today!

Enter SEREBRYAKOV, SONYA, TELEGIN, *and* MARINA.

TELEGIN. I'm not feeling too well myself, Your Excellency. That's two days now I've been poorly. Something up with my head . . .

SEREBRYAKOV. Where is everybody? I don't like this house, it's a perfect labyrinth. Twenty-six enormous rooms, people wander off in all directions, and you can never find anybody. (*Rings.*) Ask Maria Vasilievna and Yelena to come in.

YELENA. I am here.

SEREBRYAKOV. Please sit down, my friends.

SONYA (*goes up to* YELENA, *impatiently*). What did he say?

YELENA. Later.

SONYA. You're trembling. Are you upset? (*Peers intently into her face.*) I understand . . . He said he wouldn't be coming here any more . . . yes? (*A pause.*) Tell me: yes?

YELENA *nods.*

SEREBRYAKOV. One can put up with ill-health, all things considered, but what I really cannot endure is this routine of country life. I feel as if I'd dropped off the earth onto some other planet. Do sit down, friends, please. Sonya! (SONYA *doesn't hear him; she is standing with her head bowed, dejectedly.*) Sonya! (*A pause.*) She doesn't hear me. (*To* MARINA.) You too, Nanny, sit down. (MARINA *sits down and begins knitting a stocking.*) Now, friends, please, lend me your ears, as the saying goes. (*Laughs.*)

VANYA (*agitatedly*). I don't think I'm needed here. May I leave?

SEREBRYAKOV. No, you're needed here more than anybody.

VANYA. What is it you require of me?

SEREBRYAKOV. Require of you . . . Vanya, why are you so angry? (*A pause.*) If I've done anything to offend you, please forgive me.

VANYA. Don't take that tone with me. Let's get down to business . . . What is it you want?

MARIA VASILIEVNA *enters.*

SEREBRYAKOV. Ah, here's *maman*. Now, my friends, I
  shall begin. (*A pause.*) I have invited you here, ladies
  and gentlemen, in order to inform you that a
  government inspector is coming to visit us. However,
  joking aside, this is a serious matter. I've called you
  together, my friends, to ask your help and advice, and
  knowing how obliging you are, I hope I shall receive
  it. I am a scholar, a man of letters, and I've always
  been a stranger to the world of business. I can't get by
  without the guidance of experienced people, so I'm
  asking you, Ivan Petrovich, and you, Mr Telegin, and
  you, *maman* . . . The fact is, *manet omnes una nox* – in
  other words, we are all in God's hands. I am old, and
  ill, and I think it's time I settled matters relating to
  my property, insofar as they concern my family. My
  life's over, I'm not thinking about myself, but I have a
  young wife, and an unmarried daughter. (*A pause.*)
  I can't go on living in the country, it's impossible.
  We're just not made for country life. However, living
  in town, on the income we receive from this estate, is
  also impossible. If we were to sell the forest, say, that
  would be an extreme measure, and one we couldn't
  resort to every year. We need to find some means of
  guaranteeing a permanent, more or less fixed
  income. Well, I've thought of just such a means, and
  I should like to submit it for your consideration.
  Leaving out the details, I'll describe it in rough
  outline. Our estate yields a profit on average of no
  more than two percent. I propose to sell it. If we
  invest the proceeds in interest-bearing bonds, we
  should make between four and five percent, and I

think there'll even be a few thousand surplus, which will enable us to buy a small villa in Finland.

VANYA. Hold on . . . I think my ears must be deceiving me. Say that again.

SEREBRYAKOV. Invest the money in interest-bearing bonds, and with the surplus, whatever's left over, buy a villa in Finland.

VANYA. No, not Finland . . . You said something else.

SEREBRYAKOV. I propose to sell the estate.

VANYA. That's it. You'll sell the estate – that's wonderful, that's rich . . . And what do you plan to do with me, and my old mother, and Sonya here?

SEREBRYAKOV. We can discuss all that in due course. We can't do everything at once.

VANYA. No, wait. Obviously, up until now, I've been completely devoid of common sense. Up until now, I've been stupid enough to believe that this estate belonged to Sonya. My late father bought this estate as a dowry for my sister. And up until now, I've been so naive as to think – not interpreting the law like a Turk, that is – that the estate passed from my sister to Sonya.

SEREBRYAKOV. That's right, the estate does belong to Sonya. Who's disputing it? Without Sonya's consent, I can't decide to sell it. Besides, what I'm proposing to do is for Sonya's benefit.

VANYA. This is incomprehensible, utterly incomprehensible! Either I've gone out of my mind, or . . . or . . .

MARIA. *Jean*, don't contradict *Alexandre*! Believe me, he knows better than we do, what's right and what's wrong.

VANYA. No, give me some water. (*Has a drink of water.*) Say what you like! Say whatever you like!

SEREBRYAKOV. I don't understand why you're getting so worked up. I'm not saying my plan is ideal. And if everyone finds it inappropriate, well, I won't insist on it.

A pause.

TELEGIN (*embarrassed*). Your Excellency, I cherish a feeling not only of reverence towards scholarship, but of kinship too. My brother Grigory's wife's brother – perhaps you know him – Konstantin Trofimovich Lakedemonov, was an M.A . . .

VANYA. Hold on, Waffles, we're talking business . . . Just wait . . . later . . . (*To* SEREBRYAKOV.) Here, ask him. The estate was bought from his uncle.

SEREBRYAKOV. Indeed, and why should I ask him? What's the point?

VANYA. This estate was originally bought for ninety-five thousand roubles. My father could pay only seventy, so there was a debt left of twenty-five thousand. Now listen to me . . . The estate would never have been bought, if I hadn't given up my share of the inheritance in favour of my sister, whom I loved dearly. What's more, I worked like an ox for ten years, and paid off the entire debt . . .

SEREBRYAKOV. I wish I'd never started this conversation.

VANYA. This estate is clear of debt, and in good order, solely because of my personal efforts. And now that I've grown old, I'm to be flung out on my ear!

SEREBRYAKOV. I don't understand what you're driving at!

VANYA. I've managed this estate for twenty-five years, I've worked, I've sent you money, like the most conscientious steward you could have, and all that time you've never once thanked me. All that time – both when I was young, and now – I've been drawing a salary of five hundred roubles a year from you – a mere pittance! Not once did it ever occur to you to increase it by so much as a rouble!

SEREBRYAKOV. Ivan Petrovich, how was I to know? I've no head for business, I don't understand these things. You could have increased it yourself, as much as you wanted.

VANYA. Why didn't I steal? Why don't you all despise me for not stealing? It would've been simple justice, and I wouldn't be a beggar now!

MARIA (*sternly*). *Jean!*

TELEGIN (*upset*). Vanya, dear friend, don't . . . don't . . . I'm trembling . . . Why spoil our good relations? (*Kisses him.*) Please don't . . .

VANYA. For twenty-five years I've been stuck with my mother here, buried like a mole within these four

walls . . . All our thoughts and feelings belonged to
you alone. Our days were spent talking about you,
about your work, we were so proud of you, we used to
bless your very name. And we wasted our nights
reading books and journals for which I now have the
utmost contempt!

TELEGIN. Vanya, don't, please . . . I can't bear it . . .

SEREBRYAKOV (*angrily*). I don't understand – what is it
you want?

VANYA. To us, you were a being of a higher order, we
knew all your articles by heart . . . But now I've had
my eyes opened! I see it all! You write about art, but
you haven't the first idea about art! All your works,
those works I used to love, aren't worth a damn!
You've hoodwinked us all!

SEREBRYAKOV. Friends! Stop him, for God's sake! I'm
leaving!

YELENA. Ivan Petrovich, I insist you stop talking now!
Do you understand?

VANYA. I won't, I won't shut up! (*Barring* SEREBRYAKOV'*s
way*.) Wait, I haven't finished. You've ruined my life!
I haven't lived, I've never lived! Thanks to you I've
destroyed, I've annihilated the best years of my life!
You're my worst enemy!

TELEGIN. I can't bear it . . . I can't . . . I'm leaving . . .
(*Exits in great distress*.)

SEREBRYAKOV. What is it you want of me? What right
have you to speak to me in that fashion? You

nonentity! If the estate's yours, then take it, I don't need it!

YELENA. I'm getting out of this hell, this very instant! (*Shrieks.*) I can't stand it any longer!

VANYA. My life's ruined! I have talent, intelligence, courage . . . If I'd had a normal life, I might've been a Schopenhauer, a Dostoevsky . . . Oh, I'm raving! I'm going out of my mind . . . Mother, I'm in despair! Mother!

MARIA (*sternly*). Do as *Alexandre* says!

SONYA (*kneels before* MARINA *and huddles close to her*). Nanny! Nanny!

VANYA. Mother! What am I going to do? No, don't tell me, there's no need! I know what to do myself! (*To* SEREBRYAKOV.) You're going to remember me! (*Exits by the middle door.*)

MARIA *follows him out.*

SEREBRYAKOV. What's this all about, friends, eh? Get that madman away from me! I can't stay under the same roof as him! He's in there, (*Points to the middle door.*) living almost next door to me . . . Either he moves to the village, or into the lodge, or else I move out of here, but I can't stay in the same house, I can't . . .

YELENA (*to* SEREBRYAKOV). We're leaving here today! We need to make arrangements right now.

SEREBRYAKOV. Absolute nonentity!

SONYA (*on her knees, turns to* SEREBRYAKOV, *agitated and tearful.*) Papa, have pity on him, you must! Uncle Vanya and I are so unhappy! (*Trying to restrain her despair.*) Have pity on us, please. Remember when you were younger, how Uncle Vanya and Grandma used to sit up at nights translating books for you, and copying out your papers . . . night after night. Uncle Vanya and I worked incessantly, frightened to spend even a kopeck on ourselves, we sent everything to you . . . We truly earned our daily bread. I'm saying it all wrong, it's all wrong, but you've got to understand us, papa. You must have pity!

YELENA (*upset*). *Alexandre*, for God's sake, talk to him . . . please!

SEREBRYAKOV. All right, I'll have a word with him . . . I'm not accusing him of anything, I'm not angry, but I think you'll agree he's behaving rather strangely, to say the least. Anyway, I'll go and see him. (*Exits by the middle door.*)

YELENA. Be gentle with him, try to calm him down . . . (*Follows him out.*)

SONYA (*clinging tightly to* MARINA). Oh, Nanny, Nanny!

MARINA. It's all right, child. The geese'll cackle a bit, then they'll stop . . . They'll cackle, then stop . . .

SONYA. Nanny!

MARINA (*stroking her hair*). You're trembling, it's as if you were out in the frost. There, there, little orphan, God is merciful. Some of that nice lime-flower tea, or raspberry, and it'll soon pass . . . Don't get upset, my little orphan. (*Looks at the middle door, then vehemently.*) What a racket they're making, the silly geese! Go on, clear off!

A shot is heard off-stage, followed by a scream from YELENA. SONYA *shudders.*

Oh, my God, you . . .

SEREBRYAKOV (*runs in, reeling in alarm*). Stop him! Stop him! He's gone mad!

YELENA *and* VANYA *struggle in the doorway.*

YELENA (*trying to take the revolver away from him*). Give it to me! Give it to me, I tell you!

VANYA. Let me go, *Hélène!* Let me go! (*Breaks free, runs in and looks round for* SEREBRYAKOV.) Where is he? Ah, there he is! (*Fires at him.*) Bang! (*A pause.*) Missed? Missed again?! (*Furiously.*) Damn! Damn! Damn it to hell!

He throws the revolver to the floor, and sinks onto a chair exhausted. SEREBRYAKOV *is stunned.* YELENA *leans against the wall, almost fainting.*

YELENA. Take me away from here! Take me away, kill me . . . I can't stay here, I can't!

VANYA. Oh, what have I done? What have I done?

SONYA. Nanny, oh, Nanny!

Curtain.

Act Four

VANYA's *room, which serves as his bedroom, and also the estate office. A large table by the window, with account books and various papers, a desk, cupboards, scales. A smaller table for* ASTROV; *on it are his drawing materials and paints, and a portfolio. A bird-cage with a starling in it. There is a map of Africa on the wall, obviously of no use to anyone. An enormous divan, upholstered in oil-cloth. To the left, a door, leading to another room; to the right, a door into the hall, with a mat placed in front of it, so the peasants won't muddy the floor. It is an autumn evening, very still.* TELEGIN *and* MARINA *are sitting facing one another, winding wool.*

TELEGIN. You'd better hurry, Marina my dear, they'll soon be calling us to say goodbye. They've already ordered the horses.

MARINA (*trying to wind faster*). There's not much left.

TELEGIN. They're going to Kharkov. That's where they'll be living.

MARINA. And a good thing too.

TELEGIN. They've had a bit of a fright. Yelena Andreyevna keeps saying, 'I won't stay here another hour . . . we must get away, must get away . . . We can stay in Kharkov for a while,' she says, 'have a look

round, and then send for our things . . . ' They're
travelling light. Well, Marina, it seems they weren't
meant to live here. Not their destiny . . . the workings
of fate.

MARINA. And a good thing too. All that row this
morning, shooting – it's a disgrace!

TELEGIN. Indeed, a subject worthy of the brush of
Aivazovsky.

MARINA. I could've done without seeing that. (*A pause.*)
Well, we'll go back to the old ways now. Tea by eight
o'clock in the morning, dinner at twelve, and we'll sit
down to supper in the evening: everything in its
place, the way other folk live . . . like Christians. (*With
a sigh.*) It's ages since I've tasted noodles, old sinner
that I am.

TELEGIN. Yes, it's been quite a while since they've
made noodles. You know, this morning, Marina, I was
walking through the village, and a shopkeeper
shouted after me: 'Hey, you – sponger! Living off
other people!' That was really hurtful.

MARINA. Take no notice, my dear. We're all spongers,
we all live off God. You and Sonya, and Ivan Petrovich
– none of us sits idle, we all work hard! All of us . . .
Where's Sonya?

TELEGIN. In the garden. She's going round with the
doctor, looking for Ivan Petrovich. They're afraid he
might do himself an injury.

MARINA. And where's the revolver?

TELEGIN (*in a whisper*). I hid it in the cellar!

MARINA (*with a smile*). What a carry-on!

VANYA *and* ASTROV *enter from outside.*

VANYA. Leave me alone. (*To* MARINA *and* TELEGIN.) Go away, please, leave me alone, even for just one hour! I can't stand being watched.

TELEGIN. At once, Vanya. (*Exits on tiptoe.*)

MARINA. Silly goose – honk-honk-honk! (*Gathers up her wool and exits.*)

VANYA. Leave me alone!

ASTROV. With the greatest of pleasure. I should have left here long ago, but I'm telling you again, I'm not leaving until you return what you took from me.

VANYA. I didn't take anything from you.

ASTROV. I'm serious – don't keep me waiting. I should have gone ages ago.

VANYA. I've taken nothing from you.

They both sit down.

ASTROV. Really? Well, I'll wait a little longer, and I'm sorry, but after that I'll have to use force. We'll tie you up and search you. I'm absolutely serious.

VANYA. As you please. (*A pause.*) Dear God, to have made such a fool of myself! Firing twice, and missing both times! I'll never forgive myself.

ASTROV. If you really felt like shooting, you'd have done better to put a bullet into your own head.

VANYA (*shrugs*). It's strange. I attempt to commit murder, but they don't arrest me, they don't charge me – that means they think I'm insane. (*A bitter laugh.*) Yes, I'm insane, but people who hide their lack of talent, their stupidity, their sheer heartlessness, under the guise of professor, learned sage – they're not insane! And people who marry old men, and then deceive them right under everyone's nose, they're not insane, no! I saw you, I saw you with your arms around her!

ASTROV. That's right, sir, I did have my arms round her, and this is for you. (*Thumbs his nose at him.*)

VANYA (*looking at the door*). The earth's insane, that it doesn't swallow you up!

ASTROV. Well, that's just silly.

VANYA. So what? I'm insane, I'm not responsible. I have the right to say silly things.

ASTROV. That's an old trick. You're not insane, you're just a crank. A buffoon. There was a time when I regarded every crank as sick, or abnormal, but I'm now of the opinion that that's the normal condition of mankind – to be a crank. And you're perfectly normal.

VANYA (*covers his face with his hands*). So ashamed! If you knew how ashamed I was! There's no pain on earth like it, this acute sense of shame! (*Wretchedly.*) It's unbearable! (*Leans over the table.*) What am I going to do? What am I going to do?

ASTROV. Nothing.

VANYA. Give me something! Oh, my God . . . I'm forty-seven years old. If I live to be sixty, that leaves me another thirteen years. Such a long time! How am I to get through those thirteen years? What am I going to do, how am I going to fill them? Try to understand . . . (*Convulsively squeezes* ASTROV's *hand.*) Don't you see? Oh, if only you could live out the rest of your life in some new way! To wake up some clear, calm morning, and feel you were starting life afresh, that all your past was forgotten, dispersed into the air, like smoke. (*Weeps.*) To start a new life . . . Tell me how to begin . . . where to begin . . .

ASTROV (*irritated*). Oh, don't be absurd! What kind of new life can there be? Our situation's hopeless – yours and mine!

VANYA. It is?

ASTROV. I'm convinced of it.

VANYA. Give me something, please . . . (*Pointing to his heart.*) I've a burning pain, here.

ASTROV (*shouts angrily*). Oh, stop it! (*Then softening.*) Look, the people who come after us, in a hundred or two hundred years' time, and who will despise us for having lived such stupid, insipid lives – maybe they'll find some way to be happy, but as for us . . . well, there's only one hope for you and me, and that's the hope that when we're at rest in our graves, we'll be attended by visions, perhaps even pleasant ones. (*Sighs.*) Yes, my friend. In this entire district there have been only two decent, cultured men – you and I.

But after some ten years of this contemptible
provincial life we've been dragged under; its putrid
miasma has poisoned our blood, and we've become
philistines, the same as everybody else. (*Suddenly
animated.*) But don't think you can talk me round.
Give me back what you took from me.

VANYA. I didn't take anything from you.

ASTROV. You took a bottle of morphine out of my
medicine bag. (*A pause.*) Listen, if you're determined
to end it all, then go into the woods and shoot
yourself. Give me back the morphine, otherwise
there'll be all sorts of gossip and conjecture – people
will think I gave it to you . . . Bad enough that I'll
have to perform a post-mortem on you. D'you think
that's funny?

SONYA *enters.*

VANYA. Leave me alone!

ASTROV. Sonya, your uncle has removed a bottle of
morphine from my bag and he won't give it back. Tell
him it's not . . . well, it's not very clever. And I don't
have time for this. I've got to go.

SONYA. Uncle Vanya, did you take the morphine?

A pause.

ASTROV. He did. I'm certain of it.

SONYA. Give it back. Why do you want to frighten us?
(*Tenderly.*) Give it back, Uncle Vanya. I dare say I'm as
unhappy as you, but I'm not going to despair. I can

bear it, and I'll go on bearing it, until my life comes
to an end . . . You can bear it too. (*A pause.*) Give it
back. (*Kisses his hands.*) Dear, kind, darling Uncle, give
it back! (*Weeps.*) You're a good man, have pity on us
and give it back. You can bear it, Uncle, you must!

VANYA (*takes a bottle out of his desk and hands it to
ASTROV*). Here, take it! (*To* SONYA.) We need to get
back to work quickly, do something quickly, otherwise
I can't . . . I can't . . .

SONYA. Yes, yes, work. As soon as we see them off, we'll
get down to work . . . (*Begins nervously sorting out
papers on the table.*) We've let everything go.

ASTROV (*puts the bottle into his bag and fastens the straps*).
So, I can be on my way now.

YELENA (*enters*). Ivan Petrovich, are you here? We're
leaving now . . . Go and see *Alexandre*, he wants to say
something to you.

SONYA. Go on, Uncle Vanya. (*Takes* VANYA's *arm.*) Let's
go. You and Papa must make it up. That's essential.

SONYA *and* VANYA *exit.*

YELENA. I'm going now. (*Gives* ASTROV *her hand.*)
Goodbye.

ASTROV. Already?

YELENA. The carriage is waiting.

ASTROV. Goodbye.

YELENA. You promised me today you'd be leaving here.

ASTROV. I remember. I'm just going. (*A pause.*) Were you frightened? (*Takes her hand.*) Is it really so dreadful?

YELENA. Yes.

ASTROV. If only you'd stay! Well? Tomorrow, at the plantation . . .

YELENA. No . . . It's all settled . . . That's why I have the courage to look at you now, because our departure's been arranged . . . I've just one thing to ask of you: please don't think badly of me. I'd like you to respect me.

ASTROV. Oh! (*With a gesture of impatience.*) Stay, please, I beg you. You must realise, you have absolutely nothing to do, no sort of purpose in life, nothing to occupy your mind, and sooner or later, you will give way to your feelings – it's inevitable. And it's better if that happens not in Kharkov, or somewhere in Kursk, but here, in the lap of nature. At least it's poetic, it's even beautiful in autumn . . . And there's the plantation, half-ruined country houses in the style of Turgenev . . .

YELENA. You're very funny . . . I'm angry with you, and yet . . . I'll remember you with pleasure. You're an interesting, original man. We won't ever see each other again, so why try to hide it? I was even a little in love with you. Anyway, let's shake hands and part as friends. Don't think ill of me.

ASTROV (*shakes hands*). Yes, you'd better go . . . (*Musing.*) You seem a good, kindhearted person, but

there's something strange about your whole being.
You arrive here with your husband, and all of us who
had been working, running around trying to create
something, were obliged to drop our work, and
occupy ourselves the entire summer with nothing but
you, and your husband's gout. The two of you have
infected us all with your indolence. I've been
infatuated with you, and I haven't done a stroke for a
whole month – meanwhile people have been falling
ill, the peasants have been grazing their cattle
amongst my young trees . . . So really, wherever you
set foot, you and your husband, you bring ruin . . .
I'm joking, of course, but I'm quite convinced that if
you were to stay, the devastation would be enormous.
I'd be destroyed, and you wouldn't get off too lightly
either. Anyway, off you go. *Finita la commedia!*

YELENA (*takes a pencil from his table and quickly pockets it.*)
I'm taking this pencil to remember you by.

ASTROV. It's strange, somehow . . . To have known
each other, and then suddenly, for some reason . . .
never to see each other again. That's the way of the
world . . . While there's no-one here, before Uncle
Vanya comes in with a bouquet, let me . . . let me
kiss you . . . Goodbye . . . Yes? (*Kisses her on the cheek.*)
Now . . . that's fine.

YELENA. I wish you all the very best. (*Looks round.*) Oh,
who cares! For once in my life! (*Impulsively embraces
him, then both almost immediately withdraw.*) I must go.

ASTROV. Do, go quickly. If the carriage is ready, you'd
better leave.

YELENA. I think someone's coming. (*Both listen.*)

ASTROV. *Finita!*

Enter SEREBRYAKOV, VANYA, MARIA VASILIEVNA *with a book*, TELEGIN *and* SONYA.

SEREBRYAKOV (*to* VANYA). Let bygones be bygones. After what has happened in these past few hours, I've lived through and thought so much that I believe I could write an entire treatise, for the benefit of posterity, on how to live one's life. I readily accept your apologies, and I ask you to forgive me too. Goodbye! (*Kisses* VANYA *three times.*)

VANYA. You'll receive exactly the same amount as before. Everything will be as it was.

SEREBRYAKOV (*kisses* MARIA VASILIEVNA's *hand*). Maman . . .

MARIA (*kissing him*). *Alexandre*, have another photograph taken and send it to me, please. You know how dear you are to me.

TELEGIN. Goodbye, Your Excellency! Don't forget us!

SEREBRYAKOV (*kisses* SONYA). Goodbye . . . Goodbye, everyone! (*Offering his hand to* ASTROV.) Thank you for the pleasure of your company. I respect your way of thinking, your enthusiasm, your passion, but if you'll permit an old man to add just one observation to his farewell remarks: you need to do some real work, my friends, real work! (*Bows to the company.*) All the very best! (*Exits, followed by* MARIA VASILIEVNA *and* SONYA.)

VANYA (*fervently kisses* YELENA's *hand*). Goodbye . . .
Forgive me . . . We'll never see each other again.

YELENA (*moved*). Goodbye, my dearest. (*Kisses him on the forehead and exits.*)

ASTROV (*to* TELEGIN). Waffles, you might tell them to bring my horses round at the same time.

TELEGIN. At your service, dear friend. (*Exits.*)

Only ASTROV *and* VANYA *remain.*

ASTROV (*gathers up his paints from the table and puts them into his suitcase*). Aren't you going to see them off?

VANYA. Let them go. I . . . I can't. I'm too depressed. I need to get busy with something quickly . . . Work, work! (*Rummages among the papers on the table.*)

A pause. The sound of harness bells.

ASTROV. They've gone. The Professor's glad, that's certain. He wouldn't come back here for love nor money.

MARINA (*enters*). They've gone. (*Sits down in an armchair and begins knitting a stocking.*)

SONYA (*enters*). They've gone. (*Wipes her eyes.*) God grant them a safe journey. (*To* VANYA.) Now, Uncle Vanya, let's get busy.

VANYA. Work, work . . .

SONYA. We haven't sat together at this table for ages and ages. (*Lights the lamp on the table.*) I don't think there's any ink . . . (*Takes the inkwell to the cupboard and fills it.*) Just the same, I'm sad they've gone.

MARIA (*slowly enters*). They've gone! (*Sits down and immerses herself in her reading.*)

SONYA (*sits at the table and begins leafing through the accounts book*). Let's write out the invoices first, Uncle Vanya. We've let things go terribly. Someone sent in for his bill again today. You make it out. While you're doing one, I'll do the next.

VANYA (*writing*). 'Invoice to . . . Mister . . . '

Both write in silence.

MARINA (*yawns*). Well, I'm ready for bye-byes . . .

ASTROV. It's so quiet. Pens scratching, a cricket chirping . . . So warm, and cosy . . . I don't feel like leaving. (*The sound of harness bells.*) They're bringing round the horses . . . I suppose all that remains is to say goodbye to you, my dear friends, to say goodbye to this table of mine – then I'm off! (*Puts his charts into his portfolio.*)

MARINA. Why are you in such a hurry? You should stay.

ASTROV. I can't.

VANYA (*writing*). 'Leaving a debit of two roubles, seventy-five kopecks . . . '

A WORKMAN *enters.*

WORKMAN. The horses are ready, Doctor.

ASTROV. Yes, I heard. (*Hands him his medical bag, his suitcase and portfolio.*) Here, take these. Mind you don't bend the portfolio.

WORKMAN. Yes, Doctor. (*Exits.*)

ASTROV. Well, now . . . (*Makes to say goodbye.*)

SONYA. When shall we see you again?

ASTROV. Next summer, at the earliest, I expect. Not in the winter, at any rate . . . Of course, if anything happens, do let me know, and I'll come. (*Shakes hands.*) Thank you for all your hospitality, your kindness . . . for everything, in fact. (*Goes up to* MARINA *and kisses her on the forehead.*) Goodbye, old woman . . .

MARINA. You're leaving without any tea?

ASTROV. I don't want any, Nanny.

MARINA. You'll have a drop of vodka, maybe?

ASTROV (*undecided*). Hm . . . maybe . . . (MARINA *exits. A pause.*) One of my horses has gone lame for some reason. I noticed it yesterday, when Petrushka was taking it to water.

VANYA. You'd better have him re-shod.

ASTROV. Yes, I'll have to stop at the smith's in Rozhdestvennoye. Can't be helped. (*Goes up to the map of Africa on the wall and looks at it.*) I suppose it'll be scorching hot down there in Africa now – terrific!

VANYA. Yes, probably.

MARINA *returns carrying a tray with a glass of vodka and a piece of bread.*

MARINA. Here you are. (ASTROV *drinks the vodka.*) Your good health, my dear. (*Makes a low bow.*) You ought to have a bit of bread.

ASTROV. No, this'll do . . . Anyway, all the very best! (*To* MARINA.) Don't bother to see me out, Nanny, there's no need.

He exits. SONYA *follows with a candle to see him off.* MARINA *sits back down in her armchair.*

VANYA (*writing*). 'February second, linseed oil, twenty pounds . . . February sixteenth, more linseed oil, twenty pounds . . . Buckwheat . . . '

A pause. The sound of harness bells.

MARINA. He's gone.

A pause. SONYA *re-enters and puts the candle back on the table.*

SONYA. He's gone . . .

VANYA (*counts on the abacus, then makes a note*). 'Total . . . fifteen . . . twenty-five . . .

SONYA *sits down and begins writing.*

MARINA (*yawns*). Oh, Lord have mercy on us . . .

TELEGIN *enters on tiptoe, sits down by the door, and begins quietly tuning his guitar.*

VANYA (*to* SONYA, *passing his hand over her hair*). Oh, my child, I'm so depressed. If you only knew how depressed I am.

SONYA. What can we do? We must go on living. (*A pause.*) And we shall live, Uncle Vanya. We'll live through a long, long succession of days and endless nights; we'll patiently bear whatever trials fate has in store for us; we'll work for others, now and in our old age, without ever knowing rest, and when our time comes, we'll die without a struggle, and beyond the grave we'll say that we have suffered, we've wept, we've had a hard life, and God will look kindly on us, and you and I, Uncle, dear Uncle, will see before us a life that is bright and beautiful, and fine. And we'll rejoice, and look back on our present troubles with tenderness, with a smile – and we shall rest. I believe that, Uncle, I believe that fervently, passionately . . .

She kneels down before him and lays her head on his hands. She sounds worn out.

We shall rest! (TELEGIN *quietly plays his guitar.*) We shall rest! We'll hear the angels, we'll see the heavens sparkling like diamonds, we'll see all earthly evil, all our sufferings washed away by a mercy that will flood the entire world, and our life will become as peaceful, gentle and sweet as a caress. I believe it, I believe it . . . (*Wipes away his tears with her handkerchief.*) Poor, poor Uncle Vanya, you're crying . . . (*Tearfully.*) You've known no joy in your life, but wait, Uncle Vanya, wait . . . We shall rest . . . (*Embraces him.*) We shall rest!

The WATCHMAN *taps.* TELEGIN *softly strums his guitar;* MARIA VASILIEVNA *makes notes in the margins of her pamphlet;* MARINA *knits her stocking.*

SONYA. We shall rest!

The curtain falls slowly.

Guide to Pronunciation of Names

Where the stress in English polysyllables tends to fall on the penultimate syllable, Russian stress, which is also heavier, is less predictable, and this gives rise to pronunciation difficulties, quite apart from its unfamiliar consonant clusters. The following is an approximation of those names and places which might present difficulty in the spoken text, with the stressed syllables marked in capitals:

Aivazovsky	Aye-vah-ZAWF-ski
Alexandrovna	Ah-lek-SAHN-drov-nah
Alexeyevich	Ah-lek-SAY-yeh-vitch
Andreyevna	An-DRAY-yehv-nah
Astrov	AH-stroff
Batyushkov	BAH-tyoosh-koff
Grigory	Gree-GOH-ree
Ilya	Eel-YAH
Ilyich	Eel-YEETCH
Ivan	Ee-VAHN
Ivanych	Ee-VAH-nitch
Kharkov	KHAR-koff
Konstantin	Kawn-stahn-TEEN
Kursk	KOORSK
Lakedemonov	Lah-keh-day-MOH-noff
Lena	LAY-nah
Malitskoye	MAH-lits-kaw-yeh

Marina	Mah-REE-nah
Ostrovsky	Aw-STRAWF-ski
Pavel	PAH-vel
Petrovich	Peh-TRAW-vitch
Petrovna	Peh-TRAWV-nah
Petrushka	Peh-TROOSH-kah
Rozhdestvennoye	Rawzh-DYEHST-veh-naw-yeh
Serebryakov	Seh-reh-bryah-KOFF
Sofya	SOH-fyah
Sonya	SAW-nyah
Telegin	Tell-YAY-ghin
Trofimovich	Troh-FEE-moh-vitch
Tula	TOO-lah
Turgenev	Toor-GAY-nyeff
Vanya	VAH-nyah
Vasilievna	Vah-SEEL-yehv-nah
Vera	VAY-rah
Voinitsky	Voy-NEET-ski
Yefim	Yeh-FEEM
Yelena	Yeh-LAY-nah